philosophy
of religion

written for the edexcel
AS specification

Philip Mallaband

Acknowledgements

Every effort has been made to trace all copyright holders, but if any have been inadvertently overlooked Meno Education will be pleased to make the necessary arrangements at the first opportunity.

Extract from *The Blind Watchmaker* by Richard Dawkins reprinted by permission of Peters Fraser & Dunlop (www.petersfraserdunlop.com) on behalf of Richard Dawkins.

Extracts from *Evil and the God of Love* by John Hick and *The Kalam Cosmological Argument* by William Lane Craig reprinted by permission of Palgrave Macmillan.

Extract from 'The Problem of Evil' by Richard Swinburne reprinted by permission of Cornell University Press.

Extract from 'God and Evil' by H.J. McCloskey reprinted by permission of John Wiley & Sons.

Extract from *God, Freedom, and Evil* by Alvin Plantinga reprinted by permission of William B Eerdmans Publishing Co.

Extracts from *River out of Eden* by Richard Dawkins and *What Mad Pursuit* by Francis Crick reprinted by permission of Orion.

Extracts from *God's Action in the World* by Maurice Wiles and 'Divine Omnipotence and Human Freedom' by Antony Flew reprinted by permission of SCM Press.

Extract from *God Matters* by Herbert McCabe reprinted by permission of Continuum Books.

The following material is used by permission of Oxford University Press:

> p.47 J.L. Mackie, *The Miracle of Theism* (1982), p100.
> p.54 J.L. Mackie, *The Miracle of Theism* (1982), p.176.
> p.75 J.L. Mackie, *The Miracle of Theism* (1982), pp.19-20.
> p.25 Richard Swinburne, *The Existence of God* (2004), pp.130-1.
> p.26 Richard Swinburne, *The Existence of God* (2004), pp.185.
> p.28 Richard Swinburne, *The Existence of God* (2004), p.190.
> p.32 Richard Swinburne, *The Existence of God* (2004), p.136.
> p.46 Richard Swinburne, *The Existence of God* (2004), p.140.
> p.48 Richard Swinburne, *The Existence of God* (2004), pp.131-2.
> p.80 Richard Swinburne, *Faith and Reason* (2005), p.189.
> p.52 Richard Swinburne, *Is There a God?* (2010), p.86.
> p.63 Richard Swinburne, *Is There a God?* (2010), p.95.
> p.72 Richard Swinburne, *Is There a God?* (2010), p.101.
> p.74 Richard Swinburne, *Is There a God?* (2010), pp.100-1.

The following material is used by permission of Taylor and Francis:

> p.35 Anthony Kenny, *The Five Ways* (2003), p23.
> p.35 Anthony Kenny, *The Five Ways* (2003), p28.
> p.36 Anthony Kenny, *The Five Ways* (2003), p44.

Table of Contents

Contents

Contents

Preface

This textbook is for students studying AS-level Religious Studies. It has been written to cover the Edexcel specification (6RS01) Foundations: *Philosophy of Religion*.

In each chapter you will find philosophical analysis of key ideas, plus the relevant strengths and criticisms of each argument or viewpoint. I have also included possible responses to many of the criticisms upon which you can base your own evaluation. I have *not* attempted to reach any particular conclusions as to the success or failure of the arguments as that is for you to do as you work through and think about each topic.

Where necessary I have simplified the arguments, but I have only done so in ways that respect their philosophical integrity and persuasive force.

Chapter One is an introduction to some key ideas about **God** and **philosophy** that will help as you work through the rest of the book, and I would recommend that you begin by mastering some of the essential concepts that are explained in that chapter.

> ○ thinkpoint ○
> Throughout the book you will come across thinkpoints. These provide an extra opportunity to engage with the issues, to think for yourself, or to conduct some further research.

Chapter One
God and Philosophy

Introduction

In this brief first chapter, we will encounter some preliminary ideas, first about God, and then about philosophy. This will be crucial for a proper understanding of what is to come in later chapters.

Before we start we should make clear some of the key terms that we shall be using along the way. We will start with some different kinds of belief and non-belief.

Varieties of belief and non-belief

Ways of believing

- **Theism** is the belief in the existence of at least one deity that created the world (note that when philosophers talk about the 'world', they usually mean the universe).
- **Monotheism** is the belief in the existence of one God.
- **Classical theism** is the belief in the existence of a personal God who created and maintains a relationship with the world.
- **Deism** is the belief in a non-personal creator God who does not form relationships with his creation.
- **Polytheism** is the belief in a pantheon of deities.
- **Pantheism** covers a range of belief-systems at the heart of which is the belief that God and the universe are one.

Ways of not-believing

- **Strong atheism** is the belief that God does not exist.
- **Weak atheism** is the lack of belief that God exists.
- **Agnosticism** is not knowing whether to believe in God or not (or perhaps believing that whether God exists or not is unknowable).

God

When we refer to 'God' in this book, it will be the **God of classical theism**. This is the traditional philosophical conception of God that underpins the God of Judaism, Christianity and Islam. This is not to say however, that when we say 'God is omnipotent' we are committing ourselves to the existence of God. Rather, we might understand such a claim as meaning something like, 'if the God of classical theism exists, then he is omnipotent'. Indeed, an important aspect of studying the philosophy of religion is to work out whether or not there are good reasons for believing that such a God exists.

We will encounter different ways of thinking about the God of classical theism, and will need to be familiar with some key terms:

- A **personal** God is one who can (i) act in the world (e.g., through miracles); and (ii) form relationships with his creation.
- God is **immanent** means that God exists together with his creation within the universe.
- God is **transcendent** means that he exists outside the universe, separate from his creation.
- An **eternal** God has no beginning, and will not cease to be.
- An **immutable** God is unchanging.

The three key features of God's nature that we will encounter perhaps the most frequently are these:

- An **omnipotent** God is all powerful.
- An **omniscient** God is all knowing.
- A **perfectly good** God is wholly good (**omnibenevolent**). This quality is sometimes referred to as moral perfection.

There are many philosophical difficulties that have been raised in relation to these three attributes, and we will think about some in more detail.

Omnipotence

'Omnipotence' means all powerful, so at first glance, it appears that when we say that God is omnipotent, we mean that he can do *anything*.

! *However* when we say that God is omnipotent, we cannot mean that he can do absolutely anything. This is shown in the **paradox of omnipotence** (a paradox is a set of statements that, although they *seem* to be true gives rise to a contradiction that we cannot accept).

Here is the paradox:

Premise 1   Either God can make a stone that is too heavy for him to lift, or he cannot.

Premise 2   If God can make a stone that is too heavy for him to lift, then there is something that he cannot do, therefore God is not omnipotent.

Premise 3   If God cannot make a stone that is too heavy for him to lift, then there is something that he cannot do, therefore God is not omnipotent.

Conclusion   Therefore God is not omnipotent.

This argument is usually taken to show that when classical theists describe God as omnipotent, this cannot mean that he can do absolutely anything. The paradox of omnipotence shows that we would not expect God to be able to do the *logically impossible*. So God cannot make a (Euclidean) triangle with interior angles that sum to anything other than 180° because then the shape would cease to be a triangle, and neither could he make 2+2=5. Therefore, when we say that God is omnipotent, it looks as though we mean that he can do anything that is logically possible.

> o thinkpoint o
> Can you think of anything else that we would not expect an omnipotent God to be able to do? Or do you think that God can do even the impossible?

Omniscience

In the Bible (Hebrews 4:13) we read:

> 'Nothing in all creation is hidden from God's sight. Everything is uncovered and laid bare before the eyes of him to whom we must give account.'

When we say that God is omniscient, we mean that he knows everything that is, everything that has been, and everything that will be. In other words, God knows all the **truths** that there are, all the truths that have been and all the truths that will be. Because God is **unchanging** (immutable), he cannot learn new facts, so we normally think of God as possessing **divine foreknowledge**—he has always known what will happen.

! *However* according to classical theism, God created humans with free will. Now how do we reconcile our having free will with the fact that God knows everything—including what we will choose to do? Some philosophers have thought that this entails that we do not have genuine free will.

This is obviously a complex issue. For now it will suffice to note that there is neither a psychological constraint (I still have to make decisions in order to act in the world), nor a logical constraint (the fact that God knows what I will choose does not mean it is logically impossible for me to choose for myself).

Perfect goodness

For our current purpose, when we say that God is perfectly good, we mean that he is wholly benevolent—that he possesses every moral perfection. We may think of God's moral perfection as being the same as his **all-loving** nature (let's say they are two sides of the same coin).

! *However* a problem arises when we look at the world and see evil and suffering; as this makes us question God's goodness. We will come back to this issue in Chapter Four.
! There also seems to be a moral restriction on what God is able to do in virtue of his being perfectly benevolent. So, for example, God cannot change the moral status of the Holocaust so that the Final Solution was a good thing, nor can he make putting your right shoe on before your left shoe morally wrong.

> **o thinkpoint o**
> Can you explain how God's omnipotence might conflict with his perfect goodness?

The restrictions placed on God in virtue of his benevolence raise certain issues that relate to the relationship between God and morality (this is a topic you may come across in the study of *Ethics*).

Philosophy

So what is philosophy? Well we have actually already done some philosophy: in distinguishing between theism and deism, we have clarified a difference that might bring to light an ambiguity when someone expresses a belief in God—are they a theist or a deist? Philosophers work to ensure that language is used correctly, and that difficult ideas, such as God, are expressed as accurately as possible (the important 20th century philosopher Ludwig Wittgenstein) went as far as saying that there are *no* genuine philosophical problems at all, just confusion

> **o thinkpoint o**
> Find out the etymological origin of 'analysis'. How does this make sense of 'philosophical analysis'?

over the language we use). So we have been doing philosophy by analysing and clarifying the concept of God. We refer to this as **philosophical analysis**, and it is an important aspect of philosophical study.

There are some key terms that we need to be able to use as we conduct philosophical analysis:

Concerning truth

- An **analytic** statement is a statement that is true by definition (e.g., 'all Euclidean triangles have 3 interior angles that sum to 180 degrees').
- A **synthetic** statement is a statement that is true, but not by definition (e.g., 'David Cameron is the Prime Minister').
- A **necessary** truth is one that cannot be false (e.g., '2+2=4').
- A **contingent** truth is one that might have been false (e.g., 'it is raining').

Concerning knowledge

- We have *a priori* knowledge of a statement if we know it without relying on experience (e.g., 'no circle is a square').
- We have *a posteriori* knowledge of a statement if our knowledge relies on experience (e.g., 'giraffes have long necks').

Philosophers are also interested in discovering the **truth** and trying to persuade others of the truth. To this end, they use **rational arguments**. And here we see an important difference between philosophy and science: philosophy does not have an empirical (experiential) basis. Philosophers do not generally conduct experiments to back up their claims, but rather they rely on reasoning and argument.

Arguments

In order to be able to engage with arguments for the *existence* of God, and those for the *non-existence* of God, we need to be familiar with the kinds of arguments that philosophers use. We will consider three of the most important: deductive; inductive (probabilistic); and abductive.

Deductive arguments

Deductive arguments are the strongest kind of argument that philosophers can employ. They use logic to move from premises to conclusion. A deductive argument is **valid** if its conclusion cannot be false if it has true premises (otherwise it is **invalid**). An argument that has a valid structure, and true premises (and hence a true conclusion) is a **sound** argument. We say that the conclusion of a deductive argument is **deduced** from the premises.

Here are the key terms and their meanings:

- A **valid** argument guarantees a true conclusion if its premises are true.
- An **invalid** argument can have a false conclusion even though its premises are true (we call an invalid argument a **fallacy**).
- A **sound** argument has a valid structure and true premises (hence a true conclusion).
- An **unsound** argument has an invalid structure or false premises (or both).

Some philosophers will portray their arguments in a way that makes their deductive nature clear; however, the majority of philosophy is not written in this way, and the reader must reconstruct their work in deductive form. This might involve highlighting any assumptions that underlie the argument, and including them in the argument. Here we have an example of a sound argument:

Deductive argument 1 (sound)

Premise 1   All parrots are birds
Premise 2   All birds are feathered
Conclusion   Therefore all parrots are feathered

This argument is a sound argument because it has true premises and a valid structure, which takes the following logical form:

Deductive structure of argument 1 (valid)

Premise 1   All Ps are Qs
Premise 2   All Qs are Rs
Conclusion   Therefore all Ps are Rs

Whatever we replace P, Q and R with—provided that each premise is true—the conclusion must be true too. Sound arguments are the philosopher's holy grail because they guarantee the truth of the conclusion. There are many different valid structures (and you will study these if you go on to read philosophy at university).

> **o thinkpoint o**
> Can you come up with your own sound argument with this structure?

We can undermine a deductive argument in two ways:

(i) By denying the truth of any of the premises.
(ii) By denying that the argument is valid.

If we have a valid argument with at least one false premise, we do not have to accept the conclusion.

This can be illustrated in the following way:

Deductive argument 2 (unsound)

Premise 1	All kangaroos are birds
Premise 2	All birds have feathers
Conclusion	Therefore all kangaroos have feathers

This is a valid argument because if it contained true premises, the conclusion would have to be true—in fact it has the same structure as argument 1. It is an **unsound** argument because it contains a false premise (**premise 1**) so we do not have to believe the conclusion. As philosophers, we should try to avoid unsound arguments.

We should also try to avoid using invalid arguments, as the following will show.

Deductive argument 3 (invalid)

Premise 1	All humans have hearts
Premise 2	Gordon Brown has a heart
Conclusion	Therefore Gordon Brown is a human

Argument 3 contains true premises and a true conclusion, but it has an **invalid** logical form, which we can see in the following structure:

Deductive structure of argument 3 (invalid)

Premise 1	All Ps are Qs
Premise 2	a is a Q
Conclusion	Therefore a is a P

So even though argument 3 has true premises and a true conclusion, it is actually a bad argument. We can show the invalidity of this kind of argument by creating an obvious **counterexample**:

Deductive argument 4 (invalid)

Premise 1	All humans have hearts
Premise 2	My cat has a heart
Conclusion	Therefore my cat is a human

> **o thinkpoint o**
> Can you come up with your own invalid argument with the same structure as argument 4?

Argument 4 shares the same logical form with argument 3. It counts as a **counterexample** for arguments with this logical form. Argument 4 has true premises and a false conclusion; hence *any* argument with this structure is **invalid**. (Note that this is only one kind of invalid form of argument.)

We will encounter various deductive arguments in later chapters. We will evaluate them by thinking about: (i) the truth of their premises; and (ii) their validity.

Inductive arguments

Inductive arguments differ from deductive ones since the truth of the premises does not guarantee the truth of the conclusion. Whilst philosophers would generally prefer to use a deductive argument, it is not always possible to find the right structure, or to identify the hidden assumptions that would be needed for the argument to be valid. In these cases, we use inductive arguments, which provide probabilistic (less than certain) support for their conclusions. The addition of more information can increase the probability of the conclusion, but unless we have a deductive argument, we will not get a logical guarantee. Rather than deducing the conclusion of an inductive argument, we **infer** it from the premises. A good inductive argument (one whose conclusion is supported by its premises) is described as being **cogent**.

Inductive arguments are usually used to move from an observation to the unobserved. Since God is a transcendent being—existing outside the universe— we cannot experience him (at least not in the same way as we experience physical things like tables and chairs). Hence to prove his existence, which is the existence of something unobserved, we might need to use an inductive argument.

The use of inductive arguments allowed 17th century Europeans to conclude that 'all swans are white' from the premise 'all observed swans are white'. Of course the conclusion was proved to false upon the discovery of Australia and its indigenous black swans. Nonetheless, before this discovery it would have been *reasonable* to believe that 'all swans are white' was true:

Inductive swan argument

> **Premise**   All observed swans are white
> **Conclusion**   Therefore all swans are white

This argument is not deductively valid, as there is no guarantee that the conclusion will be true if the premise is true. It is also difficult to see it as a **cogent** inductive argument—even if we put ourselves in the shoes of a 17th century European. To strengthen an inductive argument we might want to transform it into a deductive one by inserting a further premise. This rarely works, as the premise is usually highly contentious and debatable.

> **o thinkpoint o**
> What is wrong with the inductive swan argument?

Nonetheless we could change the swan argument thus:

Deductive swan argument

Premise 1   All observed swans are white

Premise 2   There are no unobserved swans (i.e., we have seen all the swans there are)

Conclusion   Therefore all swans are white

Of course, the problem is that **premise 2** is false (and was false the 17th century). If **premise 2** were true, then we would be entitled to draw the conclusion.

The final option is to reformulate the inductive argument into a **probabilistic** argument:

Probabilistic swan argument

Premise   All observed swans are white

Conclusion   Therefore it is probably the case that all swans are white

Whether we would want to accept the conclusion of this argument might depend upon the number of swans that have been observed. The conclusion could have been reasonably held before the discovery of Australia, but of course would have to be rejected (along with the premise) after black swans had been seen.

> ○ think point ○
> Can you come up with your own probabilistic argument? Is it cogent?

Abductive arguments

An abductive argument is a kind of non-deductive argument that concludes with the 'best explanation'—we usually call such an argument an **inference to the best explanation**. Like probabilistic inductive arguments, they are non-deductive because the truth of the premises does not guarantee the truth of the conclusion. Here is an example:

Santa abductive argument

Premise 1   The whiskey I left out last night for Santa has disappeared

Premise 2   If Santa had visited us during the night then this would explain the disappearance of the whiskey

Conclusion   Therefore the **best explanation** is that Santa visited us during the night

Perhaps the strongest objection to this particular argument is that the best explanation for the

> ○ think point ○
> Can you come up with your own abductive argument? Is it cogent?

disappearance of the whiskey might not be a visitation by Santa. The best explanation might be different for different people. Like inductive arguments, abductive ones are used in the absence of definitive proof. Of course they can be reformulated with a deductive structure:

Santa deductive argument

Premise 1	The whiskey I left out last night for Santa has disappeared
Premise 2	If Santa had visited us during the night then the whiskey would have disappeared
Conclusion	Therefore Santa visited us during the night

However, this kind of argument is a **fallacy**—it has an invalid form (called *affirming the consequent*). In other words, we have gained nothing in trying to create a deductive argument from an abductive one. We could just as easily replace **premise 2** with:

Premise 2a	If grandpa had visited us during the night then the whiskey would have disappeared

And then reach the conclusion:

Conclusion$_2$ Therefore grandpa visited us during the night

Of course the problem is that **premise 2a** could be true, but because you know that grandpa is spending Christmas overseas, the conclusion cannot be true.

There is one way to strengthen an abductive argument, and we can show this by replacing **premise 2** with:

Premise 2b	Only if Santa had visited us during the night would the whiskey have disappeared

Now we *are* entitled to draw the **conclusion**. However, this is a difficult move to make, as we would need further explanation as to why Santa provided the **only** explanation for the disappearance of the whiskey. In the cases when this move *cannot* be made—when there may not be a good reason for thinking that there is only *one* plausible explanation—abductive arguments can be a useful kind of reasoning.

> **o thinkpoint o**
> What do you think is the best explanation for the disappearance of the whisky?

Philosophical criticism

So philosophers make us of arguments to prove (hopefully) their positive claims and ideas. Deciding if an argument is successful requires careful thought and close examination: being critical of arguments is a key philosophical enterprise, and, as we shall see, reaching justified conclusions is not straightforward. We engage in **philosophical criticism** when we question the reasons for holding beliefs, and investigate whether or not these are good reasons.

We shall encounter many different strengths and weaknesses of the arguments for and against the existence of God, and these must be considered before we can arrive at any conclusions. There are some general strengths and weaknesses of arguments that can be outlined here before we turn to the arguments themselves.

Deductive arguments

Deductive arguments provide guaranteed conclusions given true premises and valid logical form. We say that good deductive arguments are **truth-preserving**.

! *However* it is sometimes charged of deductive arguments that they do not teach us anything new—that they fail to furnish us with new items of knowledge.

! *Also* given the falsity of a premise, a valid argument's conclusion may be rejected—so the challenge is to ensure an argument contains only true premises.

Probabilistic inductive arguments

Because of the difficulty in creating sound deductive arguments, we often need to turn to probabilistic inductive arguments. **Cogent** inductive arguments provide us with new knowledge as they can take us from the observed to the unobserved.

! *However* establishing success (cogency) can be difficult as there is no logical guarantee of the conclusion.

! *Also* philosophers usually want to reach a certain conclusion, not a merely probable one.

Abductive arguments

Like probabilistic inductive arguments, abductive arguments allow us to reach a conclusion in the absence of definitive proof.

! *However* there may be different opinions on what actually *is* the best explanation.

Chapter Two
The Design Argument

Introduction

In this chapter, we will consider the different arguments for the existence of God that fall under the heading of teleological (or design) arguments. They get their name from the way that they tackle the question:

Why is the universe the way it is?

The proponents of these arguments answer the question in terms of purpose or some future goal or end (**teleological** comes from the Greek word *telos* meaning end or purpose). So the idea is that the teleological arguments aim to explain the way the world in terms of its purpose, and, as we shall see, it is supposed that something cannot have a purpose by accident. This leads philosophers to conclude that the universe is the way it is because it has been designed that way. And further, at least within the context of classical theism, because it has been designed that way by God. Note that this is a different question from that which motivates the cosmological argument, which attempts to answer why the universe exists at all (see Chapter Three).

Each teleological argument is grounded in an observation (this is how we know the way the world is). So because it is based on experience, we say that it is an **empirical** argument. Another way of saying this is that the teleological argument has an ***a posteriori*** ground.

Background

Plato

The idea of a teleological argument for the existence of a deity can be traced back to Plato (c.427-347 BCE), who, in his book *The Laws*, wrote:

'A survey of pertinent fact ... particularly astronomical data, will convince any careful observer that nature changes with the utmost regularity and that, in consequence: "There would be impiety in asserting that any but the most perfect soul or souls carries round the heavens".'

Plato thought then that the regularity we find within the universe points towards a creator god—what he referred to as the **Demiurge** (from the Greek for craftsman).

In another work, *Timaeus*, Plato also wrote that the Demiurge would have a reason for crafting such an **ordered** and **regular** world (as opposed to a chaotic one):

> 'He was good; and in the good no jealousy in any matter can ever arise. So, being without jealousy, he desired that all things should come as near as possible to being like himself. ... Desiring, then, that all things should be good and, so far as might be, nothing imperfect, the god took over all that is visible—not at rest, but in discordant and unordered motion—and brought it from disorder into order, since he judged that order was in every way the better.'

So Plato thought that the fact that we live in an ordered and regular world rather than a chaotic one is evidence that the creator/designer (the Demiurge) is **benevolent**.

> ○ thinkpoint ○
> Was Plato right to think that the order in the universe shows that the creator is *good*?

So the teleological argument has its roots in the pre-Christian philosophy of Plato. We can see Plato's influence in this passage from St Paul's letter to the Romans 1:19-21:

> 'For what can be known about God is plain to them, because God has shown it to them. Ever since the creation of the world his eternal power and divine nature, invisible though they are, have been understood and seen through the things he has made. So they are without excuse.'

This quotation makes clear the argument's **empirical** nature: we ultimately get to the conclusion that there is a God from our experience of the results of his work (Creation). We access the invisible (God) through the visible (the world).

Aristotle

Plato's most famous student, Aristotle (384-322 BCE) agreed with the idea that the world is an ordered place, but denies that the source of that order comes from outside the universe. In his work, *Physics*, he wrote:

> 'For natural things are exactly those which do move continuously, in virtue of a principle inherent in themselves, towards a determined goal ...'

This is a clear expression of Aristotle's teleological view of the natural world and the idea that purpose comes from nature itself. The particular way that Aristotle understood something's function or purpose (telos) is in relation to what he referred to as that thing's **final cause**.

Here is an example that Aristotle provided in his *Metaphysics*:

> 'The "end" of walking is health. For why does a man walk? "To be healthy," we say, and by saying this we consider that we have supplied the [final] cause.'

Or consider an acorn. Aristotle would say that the purpose of an acorn is to grow into an oak tree. This is clearly a teleological approach since we are characterising the acorn in terms of what it will become. In so doing, we refer to the acorn's final cause (to become an oak tree). This, for Aristotle, explains what the acorn is *for*.

> **o thinkpoint o**
>
> Can you provide teleological explanations of other things, both natural and man-made?

In opposition to Plato, Aristotle thought that we do not need to leave the universe in our search for final causes—as the passage from *Physics* suggests. Whereas Plato believed that purpose comes from the Demiurge, Aristotle argued that the laws that govern purposeful behaviour are to be found within the natural world itself.

The classical arguments

Within the context of classical theism, there are several key teleological arguments that we should examine. We will start with the arguments developed by St Thomas Aquinas (1225-1274) and William Paley (1743-1805). These arguments are based upon distinctive features of the world/universe, and conclude that these features prove that God exists.

Aquinas' argument from beneficial behaviour

As we shall see in Chapter Three, the first three arguments for the existence of God developed by Aquinas are cosmological arguments. His **Fifth Way** is a teleological argument based upon the appearance of **beneficial behaviour**. Here is the whole argument from his *Summa Theologica*:

> 'The fifth way is taken from the governance of the world. We see that things which lack knowledge, such as natural bodies, act for an end, and this is evident from their acting always, or nearly always, in the same way, so as to obtain the best result. Hence it is plain that they achieve their end, not fortuitously, but designedly. Now whatever lacks knowledge cannot move towards an end, unless it be directed by some being endowed with knowledge and intelligence; as the arrow is directed by the archer. Therefore, some intelligent being exists by whom all natural things are directed to their end; and this being we call God.'

We can think of Aquinas' argument in the following way:

Premise 1 We can see that the repeated behaviour of non-intelligent organisms often leads to a benefit for that organism.

Premise 2 This is evidence for that behaviour having a purpose (or end, or *telos*).

Premise 3 If something has a purpose, it must have been designed that way (it couldn't be due to chance).

Premise 4 Non-intelligent organisms cannot be designers.

Conclusion Therefore, the natural world was designed (made full of purpose) by an intelligent being, and that being is God.

Unpacking the argument

In **premise 1**, Aquinas presented the empirical base for his argument. There are plenty of examples that we might use to illustrate this point—the dance of the honeybee, the migration pattern of the Grey Whale to pick just two.

> **o thinkpoint o**
> Can you think of some other organisms that exhibit beneficial behaviour?

In order to fully understand **premise 2**, we need to appreciate Aristotle's influence on Aquinas' ideas, in particular the Aristotelian idea of **final cause**. This is why Aquinas wanted to explain the beneficial behaviour of animals in terms of future benefits: the final cause of the honey bees' dance is to communicate the proximity of food to other bees (without food, the bees would die); the final cause of the 12,000 mile annual migration of the Grey Whale is to secure survival in the rich feeding grounds off the Mexican coast. Whereas Aristotle talked of an ordered universe, Aquinas talked of a universe that contains beings that exhibit beneficial behaviour, behaviour that is good for that organism.

Premise 3 reflects the fact that we generally think that if something has a purpose—if it is *for* something—then this is not an accident. Aquinas held that purpose is only ever the product of (intelligent) design.

Premise 4 highlights the fact that natural organisms cannot choose their own ends/purposes. Aquinas' **archer analogy** is key to understanding this premise: just as an arrow will 'just sit there' unless there is someone to fire it towards a target, so non-intelligent organisms would be incapable of purposive and beneficial behaviour without an intelligent guiding hand.

> **o thinkpoint o**
> Do you think Aquinas' archer analogy works?

I have presented the Fifth Way as a deductive argument (see Chapter One), in which case the **conclusion** follows logically from the premises. At least this is true for the first part of the conclusion. Aquinas then made an **inductive leap** to 'and that being is God', which does *not* follow deductively from the premises (although this is not to say that the clause is false).

Strengths

(1) Empirical base

Aquinas' argument is based on an ***a posteriori*** premise. We do see creatures exhibit beneficial behaviour (so we would probably agree with the argument's empirical base). Arguments like this are thought of as being **universally available**—all we have to do is to observe nature, and we will see that **premise 1** is true.

(2) Valid structure

The argument has a valid structure (up until the inductive leap that is), so if the premises are true, then we should accept the first part of the **conclusion**.

Criticisms

(1) Purpose does not need a designer

If we can find a false premise in the argument then, despite the fact that it may have a valid structure, we are not forced to accept the conclusion. One premise that we may attack is **premise 3**, as Darwin's *Theory of Evolution* has provided a scientific explanation of where the appearance of purpose has come from without invoking a designer (i.e. God). This criticism is explored in more depth in response to Paley's Watchmaker Argument (see below).

(2) The inductive leap is not warranted

Even if Aquinas is right that there is evidence that world has been designed, the argument fails to give us a logical reason to accept that the designer must be the God of classical theism.

Paley's Watchmaker Argument

Foundations

In his book, *Natural Theology* (1802), William Paley developed what we probably think of as the most famous version of the teleological argument (although not necessarily the most successful): the **Watchmaker Argument**. Whereas Aquinas was interested in the way natural things exhibit beneficial behaviour, Paley's focus was the way that some natural things appear to perform a **function**.

The Watchmaker argument has its roots in the mechanistic world-view that was developed in the 17th century by such scientists as Isaac Newton and Robert Boyle. The idea of comparing the world with a watch (or clock) that appealed to Paley was then not a particularly new one. In this passage, Boyle is describing an astronomical clock found in Strasbourg cathedral, and known as the Strasbourg Clock:

> '... the several pieces making up that curious engine are so framed and adapted, and are put into such motion, that through the numerous wheels, and other parts of it, move several ways, and that without any thing either of knowledge or design; yet each performs its part in order to the various end, for which it was contrived, as regularly and uniformly as if it knew and were concerned to do its duty.'

From an artefact (i.e., something man-made) that functions in virtue of its complex mechanisms, we are led to the object's designer—the agent who designed the object with a particular function in mind (e.g., to tell the time). The clock's components behave unwittingly and unknowingly and yet in such a way so that the clock keeps time (performs its function), and this is due to the fact that it has been designed to do this.

The mechanistic view of nature then came about when people started thinking about the **biological complexity** that could be found within the natural world. This led philosophers such as Paley to the conclusion that the natural things, which perform functions (e.g., the eye has the function of seeing), do so in virtue of being the product of a designer (God).

The argument

We need to be careful in our analysis of Paley's work in order to see it in its best light (there is no philosophical point in setting up a straw man just so we can easily knock it down). For our current purposes, the best way of setting out the Watchmaker Argument is as follows:

Premise 1   We can see that a watch is functionally complex.

Premise 2   A watch is functionally complex because it has been designed by a watchmaker.

Premise 3   If something is functionally complex, then it has been designed by a designer.

Premise 4   The natural world possesses functional complexity.

Conclusion   Therefore the natural world has been designed by a designer (and that being is God).

Unpacking the argument

Premise 1 is the *a posteriori* premise that accounts for the **empirical** nature of the argument. Here we are introduced to the concept of **functional complexity**. We say that something is functionally complex if:

(i) it is made up of a number of components that all work together to produce the end result; and

(ii) it is such that if one of the components is missing, the end result would not be achieved—the complex object would fail to perform its function.

> **◦ thinkpoint ◦**
> Can you describe some other functionally complex organisms or artefacts?

As we have seen, Boyle used a description of the Strasbourg Clock to illustrate his view of the functional complexity, and in the following passage we see how Paley expressed his idea of this concept:

' ... suppose I had found a watch upon the ground, and it should be inquired how the watch happened to be in that place. ... When we come to inspect the watch, we perceive ... that its several parts are framed and put together for a purpose, e.g., that they are so formed and adjusted as to produce motion, and that motion so regulated as to point out the hour of the day; that if the several parts had been differently shaped from what they are, of a different size from what they are, or placed after any other manner, or in any other order, either no motion at all would have been carried on in the machine, or none which would have answered the use, that is now served by it.'

In **premise 2**, Paley considered that the watch has a function because it has been designed by a watchmaker. He continued:

'This mechanism being observed ... the inference, we think, is inevitable; that the watch must have had a maker ...'

Premise 3 now states that if anything is functionally complex, then it is the result of intelligent design. Paley supported this premise with the idea that **similar effects must have similar causes**—so if the complexity of a watch is due its having been designed, the complexity of any functionally complex thing must be due to the same cause (a designer) because the effect is the same. Paley explained this with an **analogy** between a telescope and an eye—an artefact and a natural object—which, as he put it:

> **◦ thinkpoint ◦**
> Can you think of any better analogies to illustrate Paley's point?

' ... are made upon the same principles; both being adjusted to the laws by which the transmission and refraction of rays of light are regulated.'

Of course Paley was not saying that telescopes and eyes have the same function, but that they both obey the same natural laws concerning the behaviour of light—and in this way there is a similarity between them. Just as the telescope requires the correct operation of its lenses and/or mirrors in order to provide magnification, so the eye is functionally complex in so far as it requires all its components (retina, iris, pupil, cornea etc) to work together in order to produce sight. We know that telescopes do not 'just happen'—we do not get a functioning telescope by simply throwing together lenses and mirrors at random—they provide magnification in virtue of having been designed, and if similar effects require similar causes, then, Paley argued, we can infer that the eye too has been designed.

Premise 4 is another *a posteriori* premise. Paley believed that we see functional complexity in 'all the organised parts of the works of nature.' He wrote:

> 'Every indication of contrivance, every manifestation of design, which existed in the watch, exists in the works of nature; with the difference, on the side of nature, of being greater or more, and that in a degree which exceeds all computation.'

The first part of Paley's **conclusion** follows logically from the premises (so if the premises are all true, then the conclusion must be too). However, Paley wanted his arguments ultimately to prove the existence of God, not just an intelligent designer:

> 'The marks of *design* are too strong to be got over. Design must have had a designer. That designer must have been a person. That person is God.'

This move involves an **inductive leap** from the belief that the world is the product of design to the idea that the world is designed by God.

Strengths

(1) Empirical basis

Paley's argument has an *a posteriori* basis. We do see functional complexity in both artefacts and the natural world. Arguments like this are thought of as being universally available—all we have to do is to observe the world, and we will see that **premises 1** and **2** are true.

(2) Valid structure

The argument has a valid structure (up until the inductive leap of faith that is), so if the premises are true, then we should accept the first part of the **conclusion**.

! **However** if any of the premises are false, we are not forced to accept the conclusion even if the argument has a valid structure.

Hume's criticisms

In his book *Dialogues Concerning Natural Religion* (published posthumously in 1779), the Scottish Enlightenment philosopher David Hume (1711-1776) weighed in with some hefty criticisms of the design argument based upon the reasoning we find in Paley's Watchmaker Argument.

The first three objections target **premise 3**. Criticisms (4) through (7) are based on the idea that even if this premise were true, Paley would not be entitled to conclude that the God of classical theism is the designer. In his final criticism, (8), Hume argued that we don't need God to explain why the universe is the way it is, and hence he starts to undermine the whole point of the design argument.

(1) The analogy is weak

Hume denied that there are sufficient similarities between artefacts and natural objects for the analogy to work. He did not want to deny that artefacts and the natural world are both functionally complex, but he did not believe that this gives us a good enough reason for thinking that nature must be the product of design. He wrote:

> 'But surely you will not affirm that the universe bears such a resemblance to a house that we can with the same certainty infer a similar cause, or that the analogy is here entire and perfect.'

(2) There are better analogies to make

Hume went on to say that the universe more closely resembles a natural organism rather than an artefact, and so if we want to base an argument on the 'similar effects require similar causes' premise, we would be more successful if we were to compare the universe with a natural organism. He wrote:

> 'The world plainly resembles more an animal or a vegetable than it does a watch or a knitting-loom.'

We should then conclude that the cause of universe is 'something similar or analogous to generation or vegetation'.

(3) Similar effects do not require similar causes

Hume argued that just because artefacts have purpose due to being designed, this does not mean that everything that has purpose must be the product of design. The mistake he is highlighting in Paley's argument is called the **Fallacy of False Cause**.

Hume then raised a number of objections, which target Paley's ultimate conclusion that God is the designer of the world. He did this by making the assumption that **premise 3** holds in order to demonstrate the flaws of the Watchmaker Argument. This is a good philosophical strategy.

(4) There is no reason to think that the universe is the result of a single God

Hume argued that artefacts are typically the result of collaboration and teamwork, and so if we are using the design of artefacts in our argument for a designer of the universe, we would do better to conclude that the universe was designed by a team of Gods—not just the one—hence the argument does not lead to the God of classical theism.

! **However** this objection violates the **Principle of Parsimony** (see p.30).

(5) There is no evidence the designer is an infinite being

Hume was an empiricist—he thought that our knowledge comes from experience. And he held that we cannot know that the designer of the universe is an infinite being because there is no evidence of the infinite within the world—we only ever encounter the finite. Therefore, there is no evidence within the world of the infinite nature of the God of classical theism.

(6) There is no evidence the designer is a perfect being

In the same way, Hume denied that there is any evidence within the world that the designer is a perfect being. This criticism too is based on Hume's empiricism: the world is less than perfect, and so there is only evidence that the designer is less than perfect. As he wrote so poetically:

> 'This world ... is very faulty and imperfect, compared to a superior standard; and was only the first rude essay of some infant deity who afterwards abandoned it, ashamed of his lame performance.'

! **However** Paley seems to have anticipated this possible objection to his argument, as he writes that a lack of perfection does not indicate a lack of design:

> It is not necessary that a machine be perfect in order to show with what design it was made ...'

(7) There is no evidence the designer is a wholly benevolent being

If we look at the world, we see pain and suffering. Hume thought that if the designer of the world were a wholly good (benevolent) being, it would lack this dimension. This relates to the **Problem of Evil** that we shall encounter again in Chapter Four.

(8) We do not need God to explain the orderliness of the universe

Hume, although he was writing before Charles Darwin, opened up the possibility for the guiding principle of the universe—that which confers order and the appearance of purpose—being, as he put it, 'a blind, unguided force' rather than the work of a benevolent deity. He went on in the same vein:

> 'The whole [universe] presents nothing but the idea of a blind nature, impregnated by a great vivifying principle, and pouring forth from her lap, without discernment or parental care, her maimed and abortive children!'

In other words, Hume's hypothesis was that the functional complexity found within the universe could have a non-teleological explanation. His assertion that it is at least possible that functional complexity arises from 'a blind, unguided force' forces us to question the very point of the teleological argument. If we could discover another way by which a natural organism could develop functional complexity, then this complexity is no longer good evidence for design. Of course, Hume was only speculating that we could explain functional complexity by reference to a 'great vivifying [life-giving] principle', but it is exactly such a law of nature that was discovered by Darwin.

> o thinkpoint o
>
> What do you make of Hume's criticisms? Do they convince you that the Watchmaker Argument is unsound? Can you explain?

Criticisms from science

(1) Darwin: the Theory of Evolution explains functional complexity

Although their theories seem poles apart, both Charles Darwin (1809-1882) and Paley were attempting to explain exactly the same phenomena: functional complexity in nature (i.e., biological complexity). Here is what Darwin wrote in his *Autobiography*:

> 'The old argument of design in nature, as given by Paley, which formerly seemed to me so conclusive, fails now that the law of natural selection has been discovered.'

Darwin discovered that in nature, organisms become more complex through a natural process—actually two processes. First **genetic drift**—when there is a mutation in an organism's genes that occurs randomly; and second through **natural selection** (sometimes referred to as **survival of the fittest**)—when those organisms whose genetic mutations have provided them with an advantage in their environment are successful, and those whose genetic mutations have provided them with a disadvantage are unsuccessful (and die out). The mutations that confer environmental benefits then get passed on to the next generation.

So it turns out that Paley was not entitled to his **Premise 3** because being designed by a designer is not the only way to produce the effect of functional complexity. The best Paley would have been entitled to is the following:

> **Premise 3*** If something is functionally complex then it has either been designed by a designer or is the result of natural selection.

But then of course, Paley would not be entitled to his theistic conclusion since functional complexity is not proof of design.

This is not to say that Paley was foolish to see design in the natural world, as Nobel Laureate Francis Crick (1916-2004) wrote in *What Mad Pursuit*:

> 'Biologists must constantly keep in mind that what they see was not designed, but rather evolved.'

(2) Dawkins

Richard Dawkins (1941-) is an ardent supporter of Darwinian evolutionary theory. In *The Blind Watchmaker* he explains:

> 'All appearances to the contrary, the only watchmaker in nature is the blind forces of physics ... Natural selection, the blind, unconscious, automatic process that Darwin discovered, and which we now know is the explanation for the existence and apparently purposeful form of all life, has no purpose in mind. ... If it can be said to play the role of watchmaker in nature, it is the *blind* watchmaker.'

His point is that although biological complexity *appears* to be the product of design, in fact it is not, it is the result of a *blind* natural force.

Dawkins argues that the empirical evidence doesn't in fact point to just one God in any case. He asks us to consider the cheetah and the antelope. It looks as if the cheetah is well-designed for hunting antelope, and the antelope is well-designed for evading capture. But why would God design these two animals in such ways? In *River out of Eden*, he writes:

> 'It is though cheetahs had been designed by one deity, and antelopes by a rival deity.'

This should be thought as a continuation of Hume's fourth criticism.

Other philosophical criticisms

(1) Ockham's Razor

See the general criticisms (p.31) for more detail about this philosophical principle. According to **Ockham's Razor**, the scientific explanation for the fact that the world contains biological complexity commits us to fewer *kinds* of entities (it is ontologically simpler) than the theistic explanation, and so is preferable to it.

(2) The problem of evil

In *Three Essays on Religion*, J.S. Mill (1806-1873) criticised the design argument along the same lines as Hume (see his seventh criticism):

> 'If the maker of the world *can* all that he will, he wills misery, and there is no escape from the conclusion.'

Mill thought that the lack of **justice** in the world was **empirical** evidence that there is no omnipotent and benevolent creator. Indeed, he held that the presence of injustice in the world outweighs the empirical evidence for the existence of the God of classical theism, and this led Mill to deny God's omnipotence.

> **o thinkpoint o**
>
> Why do you think Mill rejected God's benevolence rather than his omnipotence?

The modern arguments

The second category of design arguments has a different focus from those of Aquinas and Paley. Richard Swinburne (1934-) and F.R. Tennant (1866-1957) ground their arguments in the way that certain features of the world are well suited to us human beings. Because the arguments place us at the centre of things, we call them **anthropic** (human-centred): the world is like it is for **our benefit**. We say that whereas the classical arguments are **arguments *from* design**, Swinburne's and Tennant's arguments are **arguments *to* design**.

Swinburne's Anthropic Argument

Swinburne's argument runs as follows:

Premise 1   The laws of nature have enabled the evolution of human beings.

Premise 2   Science fails to explain why the laws of nature are as they are.

Premise 3   If the laws of nature had been designed by God, they would have allowed us human beings to evolve.

Conclusion   Therefore, the best explanation for why the laws of nature are as they are is that God designed them that way.

Swinburne focuses on the laws of evolution in **premise 1** because these laws are particularly interesting for us as they determined the evolution of human beings (*homo sapiens*).

Premise 2 is underwritten by Swinburne's belief that although science can show us *what* the laws of nature are, it cannot tell us *why* the laws are as they are. He asks us to consider the laws of evolution. He argues that science tells us what the laws are that have led to the evolution of us human beings (i.e., the laws governing natural selection). But, Swinburne maintains, science does not explain why these laws of evolution are the ones that exist rather than any other set of evolutionary principles that might have had the end result of human beings not existing.

In *The Existence of God*, Swinburne supports **premise 3**:

> 'There are good reasons why God should make a complex physical universe. For such a universe can be beautiful, and that is good; and also it can be a theatre for finite agents to develop and make of it what they will.'

There are three reasons as to why Swinburne thinks that God wants human beings to exist:

(i) God is generous and wants us to share his creation;

(ii) God wants to form meaningful relationships with intelligent beings made in His own image;

(iii) God wants us to be the stewards of nature.

Swinburne believes the **best explanation** for why the laws of nature are as they are is that they are the result of God's will (as expressed above). Otherwise, it would be a matter of **mere chance** that the laws of nature are this way, and the likelihood of these laws being the ones that hold within the universe is infinitesimally small. As he writes:

> 'So it is quite likely that, if there is a God, the laws … of the universe will be such as to make probable the evolution of human bodies.'

The **conclusion** is reached non-deductively: it is an argument to the best explanation (see Chapter One).

Strengths

(1) Scientific support

Proponents of the argument appeal to a wide range of scientific facts that lend support to the idea that there is something special about the fact that it is the actual laws of nature that are the ones that govern the universe rather than some others. This is often expressed as the idea that the universe has been **fine-tuned** (by God) to allow human life. The **Anthropic Principle** is supported by such facts as:

(i) If the force of the Big Bang had been slightly weaker, then there would not have been enough energy for the creation and expansion of the universe.

(ii) If the force of the Big Bang had been slightly stronger, then gravity would not have been able to exert enough pull to form galaxies, stars or planets.

Robin Collins writes in 'A Scientific Argument for the Existence of God: the Fine-Tuning Design Argument':

> 'Almost everything about the basic structure of the universe ... is balanced on a razor's edge for life to occur.'

o thinkpoint o

Can you find some other aspects of the universe that seem to have been fine-tuned?

Believers in the Anthropic Principle, think that God is the best explanation for all these unlikely (and essential for us) facts to obtain.

(2) The Principle of Parsimony

Swinburne believes that the God of classical theism (that is a *personal* God) is the simplest explanation for the existence of the universe. So it is not surprising to see Swinburne hold up the Principle of Parsimony as a reason for accepting his Anthropic Argument. He argues that the alternative *scientific* explanation for why the universe possesses laws of nature that have led to the evolution of humans appeals to what scientists refer to as the **multiverse**. The multiverse is a (hypothetical) collection of universes, each with its own set of laws of nature. Because there are an indeterminate (perhaps an infinite) number of universes within the multiverse, there would be a high probability of one universe containing just the right set of laws that allow human life—and that is the one which we find ourselves in. In *The Existence of God*, Swinburne applies the **Principle of Parsimony** in this way:

> '... it is the height of irrationality to postulate an infinite number of universes ... merely to avoid the hypothesis of theism. Given that simplicity makes for prior probability, and a theory is simpler the fewer entities it postulates, it is far simpler to postulate one God than an infinite number of universes ...'

! **However** we might think that ontological parsimony is more important that explanatory simplicity, and so **Ockham's Razor** can be applied (see p.31). The scientific theory that explains the appearance of fine-tuning by appealing to many physical universes is better than the theistic theory that appeals to one *physical* universe and one *non-physical* God because the scientific theory is committed to only one kind of entity (physical things) rather than two kinds of entity (a physical thing and a spiritual thing).

Criticisms

(1) Of course we see a finely-tuned universe!

There is no real surprise that we should discover that the universe supports life since if it did not, then we would not be here to comment on it! We <u>are</u> here, and so the chance of our observing a 'finely-tuned' universe must be 100% (it couldn't be other as we wouldn't be here to see it). Even though we are here as the result of a huge number of different events, what reason have we for thinking that this fact favours design rather than chance? In other words, there is no explanation to seek out.

!   **However** Swinburne thinks this objection is flawed. He illustrates his view in *The Existence of God* by asking us to consider an analogy: a madman has kidnapped a victim and has locked him in a room with a card-shuffling machine. The madman tells his victim that unless the machine draws an ace of hearts from each of the ten packs of cards that are being shuffled, the machine will blow up, thus killing the victim before he has a chance to see the cards drawn. The card-shuffling machine is then started, and to the victim's relief, it draws ten aces of hearts, and so the victim is not killed. The victim is amazed by this, and presumes that the machine had been rigged to ensure it would pick the right cards. The kidnapper reminds his victim that of course he sees the ten aces of hearts because if the machine had drawn any other cards, the victim would have been killed before getting to see any cards at all—so the victim could only have seen the ten aces. Swinburne argues that the victim is right to want an explanation—after all the probability of the ten aces of hearts being drawn is unbelievably small. Swinburne's point is that even though we would not be here if the universe did not support life, this does not mean that the fact that it *does* support life is not in need of an explanation, and the best explanation for this is God.

> ○ **think**point ○
> Think of your own analogy to explain this point.

(2) The wrong understanding of evolution

In order for **premise 3** to go through, it seems that we need to think of us humans as the *final outcome* of evolution, in which case we are best biological entities that evolution has produced. However, this gets the Theory of Evolution wrong, as we are not the best adapted beings to the *world-as-a-whole*, but rather only the best adapted beings to the environment that our ancestors found themselves in. In evolutionary terms, we might want to say that dolphins are much better adapted than humans to living in the oceans, polar bears better at surviving in the Arctic, cacti better at living in the desert, and so on. In each of these cases, 'better' actually means 'better in this or that particular environment'.

!   **However** a theist could respond by arguing that humans are made in God's image, and so there *is* something special about us that we don't share with other animals.

Tennant's Aesthetic Argument

The final argument that we shall consider is F.R. Tennant's argument based on the beauty of the natural world. This passage is from his book, *Philosophical Theology*:

> 'Nature is not just beautiful in places, it is saturated with beauty—on the telescopic and microscopic scale. Our scientific knowledge brings us no nearer to understanding the beauty of music. From an intelligibility point of view, beauty seems to be superfluous and to have little survival value ...'

His argument runs as follows:

Premise 1	There is **superfluous** beauty in the natural world.
Premise 2	Science has no explanation for the superfluous beauty seen in the world.
Premise 3	If the world had been designed by God, it would contain superfluous beauty.
Conclusion	Therefore the **best explanation** of why there is beauty in the natural world is that God designed it that way—for us humans to appreciate.

The empirical basis can be seen in **premise 1**. When Tennant wrote that beauty is **superfluous**, he means that it offers no evolutionary advantage; that it gives us no advantage and nor does it make any difference to a waterfall whether it is beautiful or ugly.

Premise 2 expresses Tennant's belief that science has no explanation of why we see beauty in the world.

Premise 3 reflects the classical theistic belief that the natural world is God's Creation, and reflects his goodness through its beauty. Swinburne supports this premise in *The Existence of God* when he writes that 'if God creates a universe, as a good workman he will create a beautiful universe'.

The **conclusion** is reached non-deductively as the argument is one to the best explanation. We should note that it is not an analogical argument: Tennant denies that we can use an analogical argument to conclude that God designed the world to be beautiful, since man-made things are ugly and polluting (e.g., cars), whereas nature is *only* beautiful (so there is insufficient similarity to ground an analogy).

> **o thinkpoint o**
> Is the world 'saturated with beauty'? Explain.

Strengths

(1) No need to deny Darwinism

Tennant accepted the scientific world-view that seems to refute the pre-Darwin-teleological arguments. It is true that there is currently no scientific explanation of natural beauty.

! **However** some scientists expect to find an evolutionary story that will explain beauty. If we are led to the 'God conclusion' simply because science hasn't yet explained beauty, we are left with a **God of the Gaps** (see criticisms below).

Criticisms

(1) The world also contains ugliness

Premise 2 asserts that the world is *saturated* with beauty. But there is ugliness in the world too: cancers, tsunamis and human misery are all natural features of the world, and yet we wouldn't want to say that they are beautiful. But now we seem to have a reason for thinking that God is not the designer of the world.

(2) Beauty is in the eye of the beholder

Some philosophers would want to deny that beauty is an objective feature of the world, but is, rather, a personal response that reflects the viewer's subjective taste.

! **However** Swinburne supports Tennant's argument by claiming that even if beauty is not an *objective* property of the world, we could maintain that God created us humans in such a way so that we possess aesthetic *taste* so that we are able to appreciate the world as beautiful.

(3) God of the Gaps

We might think that we are left with a **God of the Gaps**—a God that simply fills in a hole in our understanding that science currently fails to explain—today we think that God explains natural beauty, but eventually science will explain this, and we will then think that the aesthetic argument fails to provide us with a good reason for believing in God.

General Evaluation

General Strengths

(1) The cumulative approach

We might think that even if no one design argument by itself proves the existence of God beyond question, the arguments taken together increase the likelihood of God's existence. This is known as the **cumulative approach**. So rather than taking each argument in isolation, we should consider the different arguments together in their joint aim of proving the existence of God.

! **However**, Antony Flew (1923-2010) criticised the cumulative approach in his 'leaky bucket' analogy. He argued that ten leaky buckets are no better at holding water than one leaky bucket. In other words, a collection of weak arguments is no better at proving God's existence than one weak argument.

> o think**point** o
> What do you think of Flew's criticism of the cumulative approach? Why?

(2) The Principle of Parsimony

> o think**point** o
> Why do philosophers and scientists search for the simplest theories?

Philosophers generally believe that their explanations should be as simple as possible provided that no explanatory power is lost (in this way, philosophy and science are on the same side). This principle is called the **Principle of Parsimony**.

The **Principle of Parsimony**: the simplest explanation is the best (provided all else is equal).

Theists hold that the Principle of Parsimony supports the design argument as they argue that God is the simplest explanation of the appearance of design in the universe.

General Criticisms

(1) Kant's restriction on empirical arguments

Although he was himself a theist, Immanuel Kant (1724-1804) denied that we could use any empirical argument (teleological or cosmological) to establish the existence of an omnipotent transcendent God (that exists outside the universe). He thought the best that the teleological argument could do was to establish the existence of an architect who simply arranged matter within the universe, not a transcendent God who created the universe itself.

(2) Ockham's Razor

Most philosophers think that they should commit themselves to as few kinds of thing as possible. This is driven by the pursuit of parsimony (see above). What is properly referred to as **Ockham's Razor** is a specific kind of parsimony—**ontological parsimony**.

Ockham's Razor: Do not multiply kinds of entities unnecessarily.

What this means is that provided all else is equal, if we can explain the appearance of design within the universe without having to resort to another *kind-of-thing* that exists outside the universe (i.e., a transcendental God), then that explanation is the preferred one as it is the most *economical*. Since there are persuasive reasons to think that the appearance of design in the universe can be explained by only physical processes (e.g., Evolution), according to Ockham's Razor, it is unnecessary to introduce a different kind of entity such as God (a spiritual rather than a physical being) to do the explaining.

Despite the fact that some writers confuse the two, the Principle of Parsimony is different from Ockham's Razor: for our purposes, the former may be used in support for the existence of God (if we think God is the most straightforward explanation), whereas the latter can be used against the conclusion (if we don't want to be committed to the existence of a non-physical transcendental being).

Final Thoughts

We might think that the many criticisms raised *contra* the classical arguments of Aquinas and Paley are enough to allow us to dismiss them. And that the strengths of Swinburne's Anthropic Argument mean that there is still some life left in the teleological approach. Perhaps our position on the design argument is determined by whether we are Platonists or Aristotelians about the source of the order and purpose found in the universe. Platonists hold that this must come from outside the universe, whereas Aristotelians think that it is generated within the universe.

Despite seeing a problem with empirical arguments (see above), Kant did think that:

> 'This proof always deserves to be mentioned with respect. It is the oldest, the clearest, and the most accordant with the common reason of mankind.'

This gives us a final good reason as to why the argument is important for theists and atheists alike.

Chapter Three
The Cosmological Argument

Introduction

There are a number of arguments that philosophers refer to as cosmological arguments for the existence of God. They count as cosmological arguments because they attempt to provide an answer to the question:

Where did the universe come from?

The arguments that we shall study are all dependent upon the fact that there is a universe in existence (the word *cosmos* is simply an alternative name for the universe; *cosmology* is the study of the origin and nature of the universe). The proponents of the arguments think that this fact is one that needs accounting for, and this is what each cosmological argument is supposed to do.

The first premise of each cosmological argument is based upon an observation of the world—what Swinburne in *The Existence of God* calls 'evident facets of experience'. Philosophers describe this kind of premise as **a posteriori** (literally meaning 'after experience'), and an argument that is based on such a premise is known as an **empirical argument**.

The conclusion that the cosmological arguments aim to establish is that any satisfactory answer to the question of the existence of the universe must make reference to a being that exists outside the universe (in other words a **transcendent** being). In this respect, the arguments are used to prove the existence of the God of classical theism (see Chapter One).

I have presented these arguments as **deductive** as this shows them in their strongest light. However, as we are considering them within the context of classical theism, we will see that each argument concludes with:

'Therefore the God of classical theism exists'

Despite the deductive nature of the previous steps of each argument, this move is usually considered to be **non-deductive** (we might think of this in terms of a leap of faith rather than a logical step in an argument), and hence we generally think of the arguments as **inductive**.

The argument actually has its origins in ancient Greece with the philosophers Plato (c. 427-347 BCE) and his student Aristotle (384-322 BCE); but we shall start with the 13th century Christian philosopher St Thomas Aquinas (1225-1274) who developed Aristotle's work into his own Christian philosophy (which we call *Thomism*).

Aquinas' First Way: from motion (change)

In the *Summa Theologica* we find Aquinas' five arguments for the existence of God (his Five Ways). The first three of these are cosmological arguments, and we need to be able to articulate each of these. Here is the First Way:

Premise 1   We can see that things are in motion.

Premise 2   Nothing can set itself in to motion.

Premise 3   If something is in motion it must have been put into motion by something else (the mover), and that mover must have been put into motion by another mover and so on …

Premise 4   There cannot be an infinite regress of movers.

Conclusion   Therefore there is a first mover, and this we call God.

There is a lot to unpack here, so let's go through the argument premise by premise.

Unpacking the argument

Premise 1 is the observation upon which the empirical argument is based. Aquinas uses 'motion' in a broad sense to include all forms of **change**. So we should think of *movement* as a kind of change (we might say that movement is a change in place). Aquinas defined change as 'the reduction of something from potentiality to actuality'.

Premise 2 can be illustrated with movement: if we have a stationary object, then we would expect to see that object remaining at rest unless a force acts upon it. This idea is often illustrated with a snooker ball: the ball will remain at rest on the table, and will move only when struck by another ball that is itself in motion.

In **premise 3**, Aquinas was claiming that since things cannot put themselves into motion (nothing can change itself), things need a 'push', and a push must come from something else. He thinks that something can only become an *x* if something that is already an *x* changes it. Aquinas gave an illustration: wood has the potential to become hot (to change from being cold to being hot), but it can only do this if it is changed by something that is itself hot (e.g., a fire). And that fire is only hot because it has caused to become hot by something else that was hot.

Aquinas rejected the possibility of there being an infinite (unending) chain of movers in **premise 4**. In other words, he denied that the chain of movers indicated in the previous premise could be never-ending.

There are different ways of thinking about this point. Consider a series of railway carriages, each linked to the one in front. The carriages cannot move unless there

> o thinkpoint o
>
> Why do philosophers tend to think that infinite regresses generally fail to provide explanations?

is a first carriage attached to an engine, which does the pulling (this illustration comes from R.P. Phillips)—an infinite series of carriages would not be capable of movement without an engine.

In the **conclusion**, Aquinas concluded that the fact that there cannot be an infinite number of movers forces us to accept the existence of a first mover. He reached this conclusion by a philosophical strategy called **reductio ad absurdum**. The idea is that it would be patently false (or absurd) to believe that there was no first

> o thinkpoint o
>
> Can you come up with your own argument, which reaches its conclusion via *reductio ad absurdum*?

mover because without one, there would be no motion in the universe now, and— as the first premise asserts—we can see that there *is* motion in the universe.

Aquinas' argument relies on Aristotle's idea of the *Unmoved Move*r, (sometimes called the *Prime Mover,* or perhaps we should say the *Unchanged Changer*). If we think of 'change' as the transition from potentiality to actuality, then since the God of classical theism is *immutable* (unchanging), he is 'pure actuality', and the source of all subsequent change in the universe.

Strengths

(1) Avoiding an infinite regress

Aquinas drew on Plato's rejection of the possibility of an infinite regress:

> 'Plato held that before the many you must place the one.'

This statement really captures the principle behind the First Way. But what is wrong with an infinite regress? Well, most philosophers think that infinite regresses fail to provide satisfactory solutions to philosophical problems.

! *However* why should we think that we need a first mover? Could not an unending chain of movers account for motion? All we need to explain the motion we see in the world is the idea that things have always been in motion, in which case we do not need a *first* mover.

The problem that Aquinas saw in this sort of approach is that if we cannot get to an unmoved mover, then the regress is **vicious**: we just keep getting the question 'but what set that in motion?' without ever reaching a final answer.

It is, therefore, a strength of the First Way that it provides us with a *philosophically satisfying* response to the question, 'Where does motion come from?'.

(2) Reductio ad absurdum

The First Way has a *reductio ad absurdum* logical structure, which is a valid deductive form (see Chapter One). So, if the premises are true, the conclusion follows. That is to say the conclusion that there must be a First Mover follows logically from the premises such that if the premises are all true, the conclusion cannot be false.

! *However* the argument does not logically guarantee that the God of classical theism exists, as Anthony Kenny (1931-) points out in his *The Five Ways*:

> 'But suppose the conclusion were sound [that there must be an unmoved mover]. It would be impossible for Aquinas to go on to prove, by the infinite regress argument, that there exists an unmoved mover **at all resembling God.**'

Kenny thinks that more work would need to be done to establish that the First Mover is the God of classical theism.

Criticisms

(1) Kenny's objection to premise 2

In his *The Five Ways*, Anthony Kenny criticises the second premise of Aquinas' First Way. He argues that we humans (and other animals for that matter) can set ourselves into motion. And furthermore, Kenny thinks that Newton's first law of motion counts against **premise 2** because an object will move with a constant velocity without any external force acting upon it if it is already in motion. Hence the explanation for an object's motion need not involve an external *mover*.

Kenny writes:

> '... it seems that Newton's [first law of motion] wrecks the argument of the First Way.'

(2) No need for a *first* mover

Kenny also criticises **premise 4**. He argues that Aquinas failed to show why there couldn't be an infinite regress of movers. Kenny argues that in order to account for motion we do not need the idea of a *first* mover, but simply an *earlier* mover.

And without the need for a *first* mover, there is no need to go outside the universe to explain motion. Kenny employs this criticism against the Second Way too:

'... the Second Way, like the First, uses an equivocation between "first=earlier" and "first=unpreceded" to show that this series cannot be an infinite one.'

Aquinas' Second Way: from causation

The second of Aquinas' cosmological arguments is very similar in form to his First Way. But instead of being based upon the empirical fact of motion/change, the Second Way is an argument from our experience of **causation**. This is perhaps the most well known of the cosmological arguments.

Premise 1   We can see cause and effect.

Premise 2   Nothing can cause itself to exist.

Premise 3   If there is an effect, it must have been caused by something else (the cause), and that must have been caused by another cause and so on ...

Premise 4   There cannot be an infinite regress of causes.

Conclusion   Therefore there is a first cause, and this we call God.

Unpacking the argument

Premise 1 is the observation upon which the empirical argument is based: we see that within the universe there are patterns of cause and effect.

Aquinas then asserted in **premise 2** that nothing can cause itself to come into existence. We might think that this is also an *a posteriori* claim, as it certainly seems to be an empirical fact that we can experience.

Premise 3 follows from premises 1 and 2 since we know that there is causation in the universe, and if things cannot cause themselves to exist, their existence must be caused by something else: things need to have a cause, and that cause must be something distinct from the effect.

Premise 4 expresses Aquinas' rejection of the possibility of there being an infinite (unending) chain of causes. (See the analysis of **infinite regress** in the section on the First Way.)

In the **conclusion**, Aquinas again employed the strategy of *reductio ad absurdum* (see p.34). If there were no first cause, then there would be universe because, as he has already established, nothing can cause itself to come into existence. Since there *is* a universe, there is a cause of the universe. Aquinas then made the non-deductive move: God is this first cause.

When Aquinas talked of God as being the First Cause, this is another idea that ultimately derives from Aristotle. The First Cause (i.e., God) must be uncaused, hence Aristotle sometimes referred to this being as the *Uncaused Cause*. For Aristotle, the First Cause—itself existing outside the universe—is the **sustaining** cause of the universe, and has always been in existence (this maps on to the idea that the God of classical theism is an **eternal** being).

○ thinkpoint ○
Why could the universe not have caused itself?

Strengths

(1) Avoiding an infinite regress

See the section on the strengths of the First Way for an outline of this strength. It is considered a strength of the Second Way that it provides us with a *philosophically satisfying* response to the question, 'What caused the universe?'.

(2) Reductio ad absurdum

Both the First and Second Ways have a *reductio ad absurdum* logical structure. See the section on the strengths of the First Way for an outline of this strength (and an associated problem).

Criticisms

(1) Do we need to explain the existence of the universe itself?

According to David Hume in his *Dialogues Concerning Natural Religion* the problem with the cosmological argument is that there is no need to seek an explanation of the universe once we have explained the things that exist within the universe. He wrote:

> 'If I show you the particular causes of each individual in a collection of twenty particles of matter, I should think it very unreasonable if you then asked me what was the cause of the whole twenty. The cause of the whole is sufficiently explained by explaining the cause of the parts.'

In other words, Hume was saying that if we can identify the causes of things within the universe, there is no need to look for a cause of the universe itself, as the universe just is the collection of existing things. Similarly, if we take some cotton threads, and make them into a rope, the rope will be made of cotton. If we know the threads are made of cotton, there is no need to investigate what the rope is made of.

! *However* if we think of the universe as being an entity that exists independently of the things that exist within it, then it *is* legitimate to enquire about its cause.

(2) The Fallacy of Composition

Bertrand Russell (1872-1970) made a related point in a famous 1948 radio debate with F.C. Copleston (1907-1994). He argued as follows:

> 'Every man who exists has a mother, and it seems to me your argument is that therefore the human race must have a mother, but obviously the human race hasn't a mother—that's a different logical sphere.'

Russell thought that although we can legitimately say that things within the universe have causes, it is wrong to think that the universe itself must have a cause just because things within it have causes. The problem is that the cosmological argument is an example of the Fallacy of Composition.

The Fallacy of Composition: it is a mistake to think that the group itself must possess property *p* simply because all the members of the group possess property *p*.

! *However* there are some qualities that something possesses in virtue of the fact that its constituent elements possess those qualities. For example, if a roof is constructed from tiles, and each tile is made of slate, then it is right to say that the roof as a whole is made of slate.

(3) What caused God?

Why shouldn't we go on to ask what caused God? In other words, the argument doesn't end where Aquinas thought it does.

! *However* there is reason for thinking that the question is misplaced. Given the eternal nature of God, he has always existed, and so has no cause—he is the Uncaused Cause—according to Aquinas.

Aquinas' Third Way: from contingency

The structure of Aquinas' Third Way is slightly different from that of his first two ways. Here is a simple representation:

Premise 1   We see that things in the universe are contingent (they come in and out of existence).

Premise 2   Contingent things are brought into existence by something else already in existence.

Premise 3   If everything were contingent, then there would have been a time (infinitely long ago) when no contingent thing was in existence.

Conclusion   Therefore there must be a necessary (non-contingent) being, and this we call God.

Unpacking the argument

Premise 1 is the observation upon which the empirical argument is based. The idea is that things within the universe are **contingent**. Something has contingent existence if it is possible that it did not exist—if it might not have existed. Contingent existence contrasts with necessary existence: something has necessary existence if it cannot not exist—if it *must* exist. Contingent beings have beginnings (e.g., births) and endings (e.g., deaths), whereas necessary beings are eternal. Every physical thing within the universe is contingent.

The idea in **premise 2** is that if something is contingent, it relies upon something else to bring it into existence. We are to think of contingent things as being *dependent* upon other things.

Premise 3 expresses the idea that because contingent beings have a beginning and an end, there would have been a time (infinitely long ago) when there were no contingent beings in existence.

Aquinas' **conclusion** is that that since there are beings in existence (which is empirically verifiable), there must be a necessary being to bring contingent beings into existence because no contingent being could account for the transition from the non-existence of any contingent beings to the existence of the first contingent thing: contingent beings cannot bring themselves into existence (premise 2). Without the existence of this necessary being, there would be no contingent beings at all. The conclusion is that there must be a **de re necessary** being— one 'which contains within itself the reason for its own existence, that is to say, which cannot not exist' (Copleston)—and Aquinas made the inductive leap that this necessary being is God.

> **o think**point **o**
> Why could we not think that the universe itself is the *de re* necessary thing upon which all the contingent beings are dependent?

Strengths

(1) Explanatory force

Copleston argued that a series of contingent beings (i.e., the totality of physical objects that have existed in the universe) cannot explain its own existence.

He wrote:

> 'If you add up chocolates to infinity, you presumably get an infinite number of chocolates. So if you add up contingent beings to infinity, you still get contingent beings, not a necessary being. An infinite series of contingent beings will be, to my way of thinking, as unable to cause itself as one contingent being.'

What we need, concluded Copleston, following Aquinas, is a necessary being, which provides 'a total explanation, to which nothing further can be added'.

Criticisms

(1) Necessary beings

Immanuel Kant argued that there cannot be anything that possesses necessary existence, since this would mean that it would be a logical contradiction to deny that it existed, and 'x does not exist' is never a self-contradiction whatever name we replace x with: 'God does not exist' is not a self-contradiction, therefore if God exists, his existence cannot be necessary.

! *However* as Bruce Reichenbach points out, Aquinas' conclusion is not that God is logically necessary, but is, rather, one that 'if it exists, it cannot not-exist; as self-sufficient and self-sustaining, its inability to not-exist flows from its nature.' The point is that Kant's critical remarks target the wrong kind of necessity.

The Kalam Argument

The Kalam version of the cosmological argument was developed by Islamic philosophers including Al-Kindi (9th century) and Al-Ghazali (11th century). In essence, it runs as follows:

Premise 1   Everything that begins to exist must have a cause.

Premise 2   The universe began to exist.

Conclusion$_1$ Therefore the universe must have been caused to exist.

William Lane Craig (1949-) is a supporter of the Kalam argument, and he is committed to the idea that the universe must have been the result of an intelligent being.

In *The Kalam Cosmological Argument*, Craig writes:

> 'If the universe began to exist, and if the universe is caused, then the cause of the universe must be a personal being who freely chooses to create the world.'

The key idea is that Craig denies that the universe could have a physical cause because that would require the universe to already exist; the cause of the universe must therefore be non-physical, and given the nature of the universe (it is a hospitable place for us humans), that non-physical cause must be a *personal* being who freely chose to create this universe rather than any other (and this is the God of classical theism). Craig's conclusion is therefore:

> Conclusion$_2$ Therefore the universe must have been caused to exist by God.

Unpacking the argument

Craig supports **premise 1** with the principle that something cannot come from nothing, or to put it another way, that nothing can occur that is uncaused. Philosophers refer to this as the **Causal Principle**.

He thinks that **premise 2** is true because of the impossibility of what is known as an actual infinity. To understand this idea, imagine a library that contains an actual infinite number of books—in other words an infinite and yet a determinate number of books. There are an actual infinite number of red books, and an actual infinite number of black books, and these can be paired off. Now a consequence of this is that in this strange library there must be the same number of red books as there are red and black books combined (because, after all, there are an infinite number of red books), and yet, as we have seen, there are an equal number of red books and black books, so there cannot be as many red books as there are red books and black books (the subset of red books cannot be equal to the whole set of books in the library). Because of this absurd consequence, Craig concludes that actual infinities cannot exist in reality.

Philosopher and theologian Ed L. Miller lends further support to **premise 2**. Miller argues that the universe must have had a beginning because if it was infinitely old, then we could never get to now, to today, as that would require the passage of an infinite amount of time, and that is impossible.

If the premises are both true, then **conclusion$_1$** is logically guaranteed because this argument has a valid structure. Nonetheless, note that the conclusion of the original Kalam argument does not involve the word 'God'. We would need to make a non-deductive leap to get from the premises to **conclusion$_2$**. Craig argues that the reason for thinking that the cause of the universe must be a *personal* being who freely chose to create this universe is that the universe is a hospitable place for us humans, and the God of classical theism has the requisite qualities to make this the case: God would be able to do this because he is omnipotent and he would want to do so because he is omnibenevolent.

Strengths

(1) Deductive argument structure

We must remember that the Kalam argument was not originally used as a proof of the God of classical theism. In its original form, the argument has a valid form, which means that **conclusion₁** (that the universe must have been caused to exist) is true if the premises are true.

!   *However* a valid argument does not guarantee the truth of the conclusion. The premises need also to be true, and this is where critics can challenge the argument (see below).

(2) Scientific support

According to current scientific thinking, the universe did indeed have a beginning (approximately 13.7 billion years ago), and this beginning is usually called the 'Big Bang'. According to Big Bang theorists, the universe was born out of an infinitely dense singularity, which due to its instability exploded before starting to cool allowing the formation of hydrogen atoms initially, and then the more massive parts of the universe. The matter then started to gather together due to the effects of gravity, thus forming galaxies and stars. The Kalam argument coheres with this theory in the acceptance of the idea that the universe has a beginning.

!   *However* scientists might be reluctant to agree with Craig's **conclusion₂** that the cause of the universe is a personal being who freely chose to create this universe (as opposed to a different kind of universe). They would argue that **conclusion₂** is not supported by the scientific evidence.

In response, the theist will argue that the Big Bang must have a cause (see Aquinas' Second Way), and because there was no space or time *before* the Big Bang, the cause of the universe cannot be a physical cause, and hence must be God.

Criticisms

(1) David Hume

In his *A Treatise of Human Nature*, Hume argued that we are unable to prove that 'every object, which begins to exist, must owe its existence to a cause'. We may see this as a reason for thinking that the Kalam argument does not get off the ground, as we are able to imagine something coming into existence without being caused, and hence we have *no* good reason to accept **premise 1**.

! *However* we might agree with G.E.M. Anscombe (1919-2001) who argued that Hume's position is too sceptical. She argued that even if we could imagine a rabbit coming into existence without being born of a parent rabbit, this does not mean that we can really imagine a rabbit's existence lacking any kind of cause at all.

(2) Oscillating universe

Some scientists since the time of Einstein have considered the idea that the universe begins (with a big bang) and ends (with a big crunch) which in turn causes another big bang to occur (this is usually called the *Big Bounce* model), starting a new cycle of universe expansion and then contraction into another big crunch. According to this kind of theory, the *cause* of the universe that we inhabit can be traced to a prior physical event (the end of the previous cycle of the universe's never-ending existence). Because this model is cyclical, there is no need to consider an actual 'beginning', as the cycles continue forever.

! *However* there is little scientific evidence to support this theory—the Big Bang theory is by far the most supported model of the physical beginning of the universe.

> o think point o
> How could science tell us about what happened before the Big Bang?

(3) Quantum Physics

Although Craig thinks that the Causal Principle is undeniably true, the findings of quantum physics demonstrates that on the sub-atomic level, there are some events that seem to lack determinate causes (for example, electrons can behave in ways that appear to lack causes).

! *However* the indeterminacy that fuels quantum physics might not be a feature of the universe itself, but instead be a result of scientists' inability to accurately predict events on the sub-atomic level.

(4) Craig's conclusion is unsupported

It could be argued that although the original Kalam argument itself is valid (and maybe even sound), further argument is needed to accept Craig's theistic conclusion$_2$.

Leibniz's Principle of Sufficient Reason

A fifth cosmological argument is based on the **Principle of Sufficient Reason**, developed by the German philosopher Gottfried Leibniz (1646-1716). Leibniz held that there must be a sufficient explanation (or reason or cause) for the existence of anything that exists.

The argument based on the Principle of Sufficient Reason runs like this:

> Premise 1   The universe exists.
>
> Premise 2   If the universe exists, then there is a sufficient reason for its existence.
>
> Premise 3   The sufficient reason for the existence of the universe must lie outside the universe.
>
> Conclusion   The sufficient reason for the universe is God.

Unpacking the argument

Premise 1 is the empirical basis for Leibniz's argument.

Leibniz asserted **premise 2** because he believed in the Principle of Sufficient Reason, according to which for anything that exists, there must be an ultimate explanation for why it exists. As Leibniz put it: 'nothing happens without a reason'.

> **o thinkpoint o**
> Do you agree with the Principle of Sufficient Reason? Why?

The Principle of Sufficient Reason: For anything that exists, there is a sufficient reason (or ultimate explanation) for why it exists.

Leibniz illustrated his point in the following way: imagine a book (a geometry book) that has been copied from an earlier copy, which itself had been copied from a yet earlier one, and so on. We could answer the question of the existence of any of these books in terms of the prior copy, but, Leibniz wrote (in his 'On the Ultimate Origination of Things'), this would be less than a full explanation because:

> 'we might always wonder why there should have been such books from all time—why there were books at all, and why they were written in this manner.'

And in the same way, we wonder about the universe—especially why there is a universe at all—and this is exactly the question that motivates the cosmological argument. Leibniz went on to argue that even if the universe had been here for ever (i.e., if the universe was eternal), we would still want to find the full explanation of—the sufficient reason for—the universe. Note that Leibniz was not particularly interested in finding the *cause* of the universe, but rather its full explanation.

In **premise 3**, Leibniz claimed that the universe is not self-explanatory, that it cannot explain itself, so we must look *outside* the universe for this reason.

Leibniz then reached his **conclusion**, that God is 'the ultimate reason of things', and hence the sufficient reason for the universe. He held that God must exist (God is a necessary being): we cannot deny that the universe must have a sufficient reason, and that is God who, as a necessary being, contains his own sufficient reason and is one 'to whose essence existence belongs' (Leibniz).

Strengths

(1) The Principle of Sufficient Reason

Leibniz thought that the Principle …

> '… must be considered one of the greatest and most fruitful of all human knowledge, for upon it is built a great part of metaphysics, physics, and moral science.'

And the Principle was further supported by the 18th century philosopher Samuel Clarke:

> 'Undoubtedly nothing is, without a sufficient reason why it is, rather than not; and why it is thus, rather than otherwise'.

! *However* William Rowe (1931-) highlights an issue with the use of Principle of Sufficient Reason: the sufficient reason for the universe's existence must be such that it explains why the universe is as it is. If we say that God created the universe to be this way, we haven't reached a sufficient reason, as we would need to know *why* God created this world rather than a different one. Leibniz foresaw this line of attack, and he argued that this world is 'the best possible world' that God could have created for us. But now it looks as though God couldn't have created a different world (as his benevolent nature wouldn't allow him to create an inferior universe), in which case the universe exists necessarily. But most theists would want to say that only God's existence is necessary, and that the universe is contingent, in which case the Principle of Sufficient Reason cannot be true.

Criticisms

(1) Quantum Physics

As we have already seen, modern science, in the guise of quantum physics, poses a threat to the cosmological argument. At the sub-atomic level, particles behave in ways that are not subject to what Leibniz would have understood as sufficient explanations since the causes of these quantum effects cannot be identified.

! *However* quantum mechanics does not tell us that there are no explanations of the behaviour of sub-atomic particles, but rather that the 'classical' ones are not sufficient explanations. Leibniz himself accepts that there may be things for which we do not know the sufficient reason.

Swinburne's argument to the best explanation

The final cosmological argument we will consider is a non-deductive argument. This is the argument to the best explanation that Richard Swinburne develops in his book *The Existence of God*.

As we have seen in Chapter One, we might resort to an inference to the best explanation when we think that there is no satisfactory deductive argument to get us to our conclusion. And so the fact Swinburne resorts to a non-deductive argument indicates his concern that the deductive arguments considered above fail. We can think of the argument as having the following form:

Premise 1   The universe is not self-explanatory.

Premise 2   If God existed then this would explain why the universe exists.

Premise 3   There are no other plausible explanations of why the universe exists.

Conclusion   Therefore the best explanation of why the universe exists is God.

Unpacking the argument

In **premise 1** Swinburne is making the same point as Leibniz: that the explanation for why the universe exists cannot be found within the universe.

Swinburne believes that there is good reason for holding **premise 2**. As we have seen in Chapter Two, he argues that there are good reasons for thinking that the God of classical theism would want human beings to exist. And because human beings have a physical body, we need a physical universe in which to live. Hence God would need to create a universe like the one we find ourselves in.

In **premise 3**, Swinburne is claiming that the theist's explanation of the universe is the only one that offers a genuine explanation for why the universe exists. He argues that atheistic accounts (i.e., scientific theories) fail to explain why the universe exists:

'If we confine ourselves to scientific explanation, it will now follow that the existence of the universe … has no explanation.'

He holds that whilst science can tell us about the creation of the universe (the Big Bang theory for example), it fails to tell us why the universe was created.

In the **conclusion**, we see why the argument is *inductive* in nature: Swinburne is not concluding that God must exist, but rather that God is the most likely reason for the universe. The lack of a logical guarantee is expressed in this passage:

> '... theism is perhaps very unlikely, but it is far more likely than any rival supposition. Hence [the existence of the universe is] substantial evidence for the truth of theism.'

Swinburne thinks of his argument as providing a *personal explanation* of the universe. By this he means that it is 'an explanation given in terms of a person who is not part of the universe acting from without.' A personal God *acting intentionally* is, according to Swinburne, the **simplest** explanation for the existence of the universe, in which case—due to the Principle of Parsimony (see Chapter Two)—the **best explanation** of the universe is that God created the universe on purpose.

Strengths

(1) Inductive argument

The fact that Swinburne's argument is inductive, rather than deductive makes it easier to accept since there is no attempt to logically prove (and hence prove without question) the existence of God. The modest conclusion that he draws (i.e., that God is the most likely explanation for the universe) looks attractive especially given the lack of possible alternative explanations.

Criticisms

(1) Ockham's Razor

Ockham's Razor can be applied to resist Swinburne's conclusion (see p.49).

(2) God's existence is unlikely

J.L. Mackie (1917-81) accepted that Swinburne is right to argue that a personal God would explain the existence of the universe. However, he thought that Swinburne failed to take into account the fact that God's existence is very unlikely. As he wrote in *The Miracle of Theism*:

> '... the hypothesis of divine creation *is* very unlikely.'

Mackie argued that Swinburne is wrong to think of God as the best explanation of the existence of the universe because of what he saw as the implausibility of the belief that the God of classical theism exists.

> o think**point** o
> What do you think is the best explanation for the existence of the universe? Can you explain?

(3) False dichotomy

We can see a problem with Swinburne's argument in this passage from *The Existence of God*:

> 'It is very unlikely that a universe would exist uncaused, but rather more likely that God would exist uncaused. The existence of the universe … can be made comprehensible if we suppose that it is brought about by God.'

Swinburne is presenting a false choice: either (i) the universe is uncaused; or (ii) the universe is caused by an uncaused personal God. There seems to be no good reason to think that there could not be a cause of the universe that is *not* a personal God. David Hume thought that the evidence of the universe fails to make monotheism any more likely than polytheism.

! *However* Swinburne counters Hume's criticism using the **Principle of Parsimony** (see below). He argues that monotheism is a simpler explanation of the uniformity found in the universe than is polytheism (this links with his design argument—see Chapter Two). In *The Existence of God* he writes, 'a God of infinite power, knowledge, and freedom is the … simplest kind of person which there could be.'

General Evaluation

General strengths

(1) Why does the universe exist?

It is certainly true that we, as inquisitive rational beings, want an answer to the questions of 'why is the universe in existence?' and 'where did the universe come from?'. The cosmological argument provides an answer to these perennial problems.

(2) Principle of Parsimony

> o thinkpoint o
> Why do philosophers and scientists search for the simplest theories?

Swinburne thinks that according to this philosophical principle (see p.30), the Cosmological Argument is a success. He writes:

'God is simpler than anything we can imagine and gives a simple explanation for the system [i.e., the universe].'

! *However* it could be countered that God is not a simple explanation for the universe, as we would need a further explanation of how a being existing outside of time and space could cause something physical to exist (and that is not going to be a simple explanation).

General criticisms

(1) Ockham's Razor

If we can explain the existence of the universe satisfactorily without having to resort to another *kind-of-thing* that exists outside the universe (i.e., a transcendental God), then that explanation is the preferred one as it is the most *economical* according to Ockham's Razor (see p.31). John Hick (1922-2012) wrote,

> 'The atheistic option that the universe is "just there" is the more economical option.'

! *However* Hick didn't think that we should use Ockham's Razor to deny God's existence, but rather that sometimes ontological parsimony is not the deciding factor: theists will believe that the appeal to God in order to explain the universe is essential, and definitely not unnecessary, therefore the less economical theory is the preferred one.

Again, we should note that despite the fact that some writers confuse the two, the Principle of Parsimony is different from Ockham's Razor: for our purposes, the former may be used in support for the existence of God (if we think God is the most straightforward explanation), whereas the latter can be used against the conclusion (if we don't want to be committed to the existence of a non-physical transcendental being).

(2) Leap of Faith

All of the cosmological arguments end with a non-deductive **leap of faith** to the conclusion that God exists (at least when used by theists). There is no logical guarantee for this move, and we would need independent reasons to support the claim that the cause of (or sufficient reason for) the universe is indeed the God of classical theism.

Final thoughts

In his debate with Copleston, Russell described the existence of the universe as a **brute fact**—a fact that does not require explanation. He proposed that the universe is 'just there, and that's all'. Copleston thought that Russell was just trying to duck out of the debate, and accused him of trying to avoid engaging with the argument:

> 'If one refuses to even sit down at the chess board and make a move, one cannot, of course, be checkmated.'

But Russell refused to be drawn in as he denied that the existence of the universe is something that requires explanation. He accused Copleston's board as being 'skewed'—if you follow the reasoning of the cosmological argument, yes, you will end up with God, but (and this is Russell's point) we shouldn't set off on the journey in the first place.

We will close this chapter with this poetic expression of Russell's scepticism:

> '[A] physicist looks for causes; that does not necessarily imply that there are causes everywhere. A man may look for gold without assuming that there is gold everywhere; if he finds gold, well and good, if he doesn't he's had bad luck. The same is true when the physicists look for causes.'

Chapter Four
Evil and Suffering

Introduction

In this chapter, we will investigate the issues surrounding evil and suffering for religious believers. We will start by considering what the problem of evil itself is, and why evil and suffering is problematic for theists, before going on to consider and evaluate some of the responses to the problem that have been formulated.

What is evil?

We may start with a definition of evil from John Hick, who wrote that evil is 'physical pain, mental suffering and moral wickedness'. This is a neat definition, although we should be careful not to include pins and needles, or the feeling you get when you lose your keys as manifestations of evil. In 'God, Evil, and Suffering', Daniel Howard-Snyder focuses on

> '... undeserved, intense suffering and pain as well as horrific wickedness. I'm not interested here in suffering that people deserve, or in bumps and bruises or white lies and mild temper tantrums. I will focus on the stuff that turns our stomachs.'

We can then think of evil as undeserved suffering and pain. In other words, evil is that which causes **gratuitous** and **intense** suffering to the innocent.

Two kinds of evil

Philosophers usually distinguish between two categories of evil:

Moral evil   that which causes undeserved and intense suffering as the result of human choices and actions (e.g., the Holocaust, murder and torture).

Natural evil   that which causes undeserved and intense suffering and is not due to our actions (e.g., hurricanes, tsunamis, earthquakes).

There may be some evils that are difficult to categorise. Take famine for example: lack of sufficient rain is a natural phenomenon, but then if the developed countries dropped the debts of the less economically developed countries that suffer famine due to lack of rain, those LEDCs might be able to build up an infrastructure such that the lack of rain does not cause famine on such a huge scale as has recently been seen especially in countries such as Sudan and Ethiopia. Indeed, in his *Is There a God?*, Swinburne classifies famine as a moral evil because it results from 'humans negligently failing to do what they ought to do'. Similarly, whilst the 2005 hurricane Katrina was a natural event, if the increase in unpredictable and freakish weather patterns is a result of global warming, then humans have a hand in the ensuing pain and suffering, and we might want to classify the environmental impact of global warming as the result of moral evil.

> **○ thinkpoint ○**
> Assuming that natural disasters can cause pain and suffering, would we want to say that such events are evil? Why?

The problems of evil

We are not here so concerned with what might be thought of as the **practical problem** of evil—that is what should we do when we encounter suffering (perhaps the rather obvious answer to this question is that we should try to relieve it). Rather, we will think about the particular **philosophical problems** faced by theists (believers in the God of classical theism). Before turning to these, we will take a quick look at a religious problem that the existence of evil might pose a problem for a theist.

Religious problem: faith

A pressing problem that arises from the presence of evil and suffering is how to maintain faith in God in the face of evil and suffering. In *God, Freedom, and Evil*, Alvin Plantinga (1932-) describes how this problem may be felt:

> 'The theist may find a *religious* problem in evil; in the presence of his own suffering or that of someone near to him he may find it difficult to maintain what he takes to be the proper attitude towards God. Faced with great personal suffering or misfortune, he may be tempted to rebel against God, to shake his fist in God's face, or even to give up belief in God altogether… Such a problem calls, not for philosophical enlightenment, but for pastoral care.'

This is a *religious* problem rather than a *philosophical* one, and we won't really say much more about it—except that if the latter can be solved, this might provide an individual with the framework for addressing the issue of faith.

Philosophical problem 1: the inconsistent triad

As we saw in Chapter One, theists conceive of God as having the following three qualities:

(i) Omnipotence (God is all powerful)

(ii) Omniscience (God is all knowing)

(iii) Benevolence (God is perfectly good)

But, how are we to reconcile this conception of God with the fact that evil exists? The problem arises because of the implications of this characterisation of God:

(i) If God is omnipotent then he has the power to prevent evil and suffering.

(ii) If God is omniscient then he knows (a) that people suffer; and (b) how to prevent this suffering.

(iii) If God is benevolent then he would not want us to suffer.

So this is the problem: it looks as if the presence of evil in the world is *incompatible* with the existence of the God of classical theism because that God seems to possess qualities that mean that he has the power and goodness to prevent evil and suffering. The essence of the problem was recognised by Augustine in his book *Confessions*:

> 'Either God is not able to abolish evil or not willing; if he is not able then he is
> not all-powerful, if he is not willing then he is not all-good.'

Augustine, as we shall see, sought a theistic solution to this problem of evil, but other philosophers have seen the problem as presenting theism with a devastating challenge. One such was J.L. Mackie who, in 'Evil and Omnipotence', argued that the problem of evil poses a serious threat to classical theism.

The problem, which we know as Mackie's **Inconsistent Triad** is that one *cannot* believe that God is both omnipotent (this is taken to include his being omniscient) and benevolent whilst also believing that there is evil and suffering in the world because the three propositions pose a **logical contradiction**— this is to say that the laws of logic dictate that the three sentences of the triad cannot all be true.

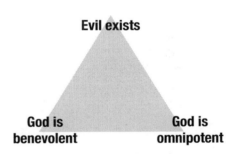

This is a deductive argument for the non-existence of God because it relies on logic to move from the premises to the conclusion that God does not exist.

In 'God and Evil', H.J. McCloskey summarised this problem neatly:

o thinkpoint o
Which of the three propositions do you think a theist would be willing to dismiss as being false?

'Evil is a problem for the theist in that a contradiction is involved in the fact of evil on the one hand, and the belief in the omnipotence and perfection of God on the other.'

We may present Mackie's argument formally as follows:

Premise 1 If an omnipotent and benevolent God exists then there would be no evil and suffering in the world

Premise 2 There is evil and suffering in the world

Conclusion Therefore it is not the case that an omnipotent and benevolent God exists

Mackie saw his argument as attacking traditional ideas underlying classical theism, and in *The Miracle of Theism* he concluded that:

'… theism cannot be made coherent without a serious change in at least one of its central doctrines.'

This would require, Mackie thought, a different attitude to either the idea of God's goodness, or the idea of God's power. Either way, God's existence could only be rescued by rejecting at least one quality normally ascribed to him by classical theism.

Philosophical problem 2: evidence for the non-existence of God

There are, however, other ways of thinking about the problem of evil. Some philosophers think that the presence of evil and suffering just makes it more likely (or more probable) that there is no God of classical theism, rather than proving the non-existence of God beyond doubt. This kind of argument is sometimes called the **evidential** or **inductive** argument for the non-existence of God because the presence of evil is used as evidence in an inductive argument for the non-existence of God.

According to William Rowe, there is no logical contradiction in believing both that there is evil in the world and that God exists. He argues that theism cannot adequately explain *why* there is evil in the world, and so the presence of evil makes it more probable that there is no God—in other words, the atheist's explanation of the existence of evil is more likely that the theist's.

In very basic terms, we might think of Rowe's argument in the following way:

Premise 1   There are cases of gratuitous evil that an omnipotent and omniscient God would have been able to prevent (without causing a greater evil in doing so).

Premise 2   It is likely that a benevolent God would want to prevent such gratuitous evil.

Conclusion   Therefore it is unlikely that there is an omnipotent, omniscient and benevolent God.

The argument is inductive because Rowe thinks that the premises do not give a logical proof of the non-existence of God, but merely are good grounds for thinking that God's existence is unlikely. He illustrates his argument in the following way: consider that there is a fawn that dies slowly and painfully in a forest fire. We would expect both that (i) an omnipotent and omniscient God would have been able to prevent this pointless suffering; and (ii) a benevolent God would want to prevent this kind of suffering as it seems to serve no purpose.

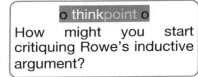

o thinkpoint o

How might you start critiquing Rowe's inductive argument?

In 'The Problem of Evil and Some Varieties of Atheism', Rowe concludes that:

'… it does seem that we have *rational support* for atheism, that it is reasonable to believe that the theistic God does not exist.'

How to solve the problem of evil and suffering

There are a range of possible solutions open to us if we want to hang on to a belief in God in the face of evil and suffering. We will quickly race through three, before focussing on the fourth.

Possible solution 1: denial of God's qualities

One way to maintain faith in God is simply to deny that he has all three of the qualities normally attributed to him, and actually he is not able to prevent evil and suffering. So one of the following denials could be made:

Denial 1   **God is not omnipotent** in which case God is incapable of preventing evil and suffering

Denial 2   **God is not wholly good** in which case God has no desire to see an end of our suffering

This approach can be thought as a reaction to both Mackie's Inconsistent Triad and Rowe's inductive argument. We could either follow J.S. Mill by accepting denial 1 (see Mill's criticism of the design argument in Chapter Two), or reject God's benevolence. Either way, the problem of evil disappears, although we are left with a religious problem: why would we worship a God that is incapable of preventing evil and suffering, or one that has no desire to see an end to suffering?

Possible solution 2: qualification of God's nature

So perhaps we want to maintain that God is wholly good, but what this means is something different from what we had previously thought—such that the fact that God is benevolent does not mean that he wants to see an end to our suffering. In other words, we previously thought that God's love for us was like our love for each other, but in fact it is very different, and is the kind of love that allows loved ones to be subject to evil and suffering.

Or we might want to say that God is omnipotent, but this does not mean that God can do absolutely anything: he cannot, for example, create a rock that is too heavy for him to lift (we considered this paradox in Chapter One), and similarly, he cannot prevent evil and suffering.

! **However** the problem with this approach, as Antony Flew pointed out, is that by changing the nature of God in the face of the problem of evil, we qualify his nature such that God ...

> '... dies the death of a thousand qualifications.'

What this means is that we end up with a deity that bears no resemblance to the God of classical theism, and another religious problem: what *is* the nature of the God we are worshipping?

Possible solution 3: Deny the existence of evil and suffering

Another alternative is to deny the reality of evil and suffering—to say that it is not true that evil and suffering exist as real entities in the world. It appears that this is the view held by Christian Science. In *Science and Health with Key to the Scriptures*, Mary Baker Eddy, the founder of Christian Science, argued that evil is in fact an illusion, and is not a genuine feature of the world. Christian Science teaches that what we see as evil is actually just a lack of goodness. We will encounter this important idea again in Augustine's attempted solution to the problem of evil.

! **However** this seems a difficult position to maintain given that we often do suffer (to some degree), and thus we have direct knowledge of suffering. Perhaps the way to go is to argue that although **suffering** is real, there is no such thing as **evil**. Of course we might choose to define evil as that which causes suffering, in which case the existence of suffering guarantees the existence of evil, but someone might want to say that suffering can occur without evil. Such a person might deny the existence of **natural evil** for just this reason (they might say that volcanoes are not *evil* even though they do cause suffering).

Possible solution 4: Theodicies

What theists need is a way to explain why an all powerful, all loving God allows evil to persist even though he loves us and is able to stop our suffering; why the three statements in Mackie's Inconsistent Triad are in fact compatible, and why Rowe's argument does not increase the likelihood that God does not exist.

This kind of possible solution is called a **theodicy**, and we will consider two such theories—first that of St Augustine of Hippo (3rd/4th century Christian philosopher and theologian), and second the theodicy of St Irenaeus (2nd century Christian theologian). The key idea behind a theodicy is that it does not qualify God's nature, but rather justifies the existence of evil and suffering in light of that nature.

Augustinian theodicy

Augustine's theodicy is based upon the story of Creation as found in the book of Genesis. In his work *Confessions*, Augustine maintained that God created a perfect world:

> 'I saw and it was made clear to me that you [God] made all things good.'

And, as we read in the book of Genesis, the paradise (the Garden of Eden) was only spoiled when Adam and Eve chose to turn away from God by going against his will and taking fruit from the tree of the knowledge of good and evil (Genesis 3). This episode is named the **Fall of Man** as it is when humans fell from God's grace. It is at this point that, according to Augustine, evil was created—not by God—but by humans and the angels that chose to go against God's will through their own **free will** and commit what Augustine referred to as **Original Sin**.

> o thinkpoint o
> Find out more about the Fall in the book of Genesis, chapters 1-3.

Augustine agreed with St Paul who wrote that 'sin entered the world through one man' (Romans 5:12). This means that human nature was changed by the Fall, and that all of Adam's descendants would then be born in sin. Augustine explained this by arguing that we were **seminally present** in Adam; hence we have inherited the punishments that God delivered (pain during childbirth and subservience to her husband for Eve, and hard work in the fields for Adam).

Augustine believed that Original Sin is passed through the generations because we are born as the product of lust (sexual desire), which Augustine considered to be a sin as it leads us away from God (a sin is committed when we turn away from God).

Furthermore, we continue to use our free will to choose to turn away from God and so we deserve **punishment**. Since God is **just**, he punishes us accordingly, as Augustine wrote:

> '… the free choice of the will is the reason why we do wrong and suffer your just judgement.'

Rather than thinking of evil as a substance or entity (e.g., Satan), Augustine conceived of evil as a **privation** (a lack or absence) of goodness (we sometimes use the Latin: *privatio boni*). So just as blindness is a lack of sight, evil is a lack of goodness. In *God Matters*, Herbert McCabe (1926-2001) wrote:

> 'If I have a hole in my sock, the hole is not anything at all, it is just an absence of wool or cotton or whatever, but it is a perfectly real hole in my sock. … *Nothing* in the wrong place can be just as real and just as important as *something* in the wrong place.'

So, according to Augustine, evil is not an entity created by God. **Moral evil** is rooted in our choosing to turn away from God, and is thus the result of our **free will**. **Natural evil**, Augustine believed, was also brought about by the Fall and stems from the corruption of the natural world that was caused by Original Sin. Before the Fall, the world was a paradise, and afterwards, due to the choices made by Adam and Eve, it became a world plagued by earthquakes, tsunamis and disease (privations of goodness).

Augustine's theory is a **soul deciding-theodicy**, a way of distinguishing between those who might deserve heaven upon their death, and those who do not. Augustine believed that there is a way to free ourselves from sin, after all God is benevolent (Augustine did not want to deny that God loves us—denying God's benevolence would not be consistent with the aims of a theodicy). We can achieve redemption for our sins by accepting Jesus Christ as our saviour. As Augustine wrote:

> '... in Christ your Son our Lord ... you have provided a way of salvation whereby humanity can come to the future life after death.'

Strengths

(1) Biblical support

The theodicy coheres with the book of Genesis, and so will appeal to those theists (Creationists) who hold that this book should be taken to be literally true.

! **However** if Augustine's theodicy is only acceptable to Creationists, then it will be limited in its appeal as there are many theists who take the book of Genesis to be a myth rather than a report of literal fact.

In response to this, we might argue that the key idea in Augustine's theodicy is that God punishes those who sin because he is **just**. So humans suffer because we misuse our free will, and this need not be tracked back to the *first* time a human freely chose to go against God's will.

(2) Free will

The fact that humans have **free will** has a central role in Augustine's theodicy, and in particular, the idea that we are able to choose between right and wrong seems to be a true reflection of how choosing often feels to us. We do indeed sometimes do the wrong the thing even though we know it *is* the wrong thing to do. In other words, the fact that something is wrong is not always enough to ensure that we don't do it due to our having free will. Augustine's theodicy seems to do justice to this important concept.

(3) No qualification of God's nature

If we accept Augustine's theodicy, there is no need to qualify God's nature in the face of evil and suffering: there need be no limit placed on his omnipotence as evil is not something that was created by God; and no limit need be placed on his benevolence as God's love for humanity is expressed through the redemption that can be achieved through Jesus.

Criticisms

(1) A logical problem

The German philosopher Friedrich Schleiermacher (1768-1834) argued that there is a logical contradiction in Augustine's theodicy: if God had created a perfect world, then how could evil have appeared in the world? It would have to have come from nothing—**ex nihilo**—and, as we know from science, nothing can come from nothing.

Schleiermacher thought that Augustine would have to reject the idea that God is not to blame for evil and suffering, and accept that either:

(i) God made an imperfect world (that already contained evil); or

(ii) God caused evil to appear at some point after the Creation.

In either case, according to Schleiermacher, evil is the not the fault of humans misusing their free will.

! **However** we should remember that for Augustine, evil is simply a lack of good, so the Fall does not rely on evil being created out of nothing, but instead it relies on, we might say, 'some goodness being lost'.

(2) A problem of choice

A related problem is this: if we were to accept the key Augustinian claim that the world in which Adam and Eve found themselves was perfect, how could they have *chosen* evil over good in the first place? The problem seems to lie in Augustine's literal interpretation of Genesis 2:

> 'And the LORD God commanded the man, "You are free to eat from any tree in the garden; but you must not eat from the tree of the knowledge of good and evil, for when you eat of it you will surely die.'

In other words, if there was no evil, then how could Adam and Eve have chosen evil over good?

! **However** again we need to remember that for Augustine, evil is simply a lack of good, so the Fall does not rely on Adam and Eve choosing evil over good, but rather choosing a *lack of good* over good.

But there still seems to be an inconsistency since Augustine believed that 'God has made all things very good'. The problem is that if Augustine is right that everything was good before the Fall, then there is no *lack of good* for Adam and Eve to choose in the first place.

(3) Moral problems

There seems to be a moral criticism of Augustine's theodicy that we can make: it just does not seem fair or just to punish us for something our ancestors (allegedly) did. And neither would we want to say that the pleasure taken from sex is in itself

> **o thinkpoint o**
> What is the relationship between justice and benevolence?

a bad thing (this is not to say however that the pleasure a rapist might have is a good thing). Further still, given God's omniscience, he knew that we would sin, and he prepared a punishment for us: Hell. This does not sound like a benevolent God.

(4) The problem of natural evil

The final point that we should consider is how does the Augustinian theodicy explain the existence of natural evil? We might be able to see how *moral evil* is the result of humans abusing their free will, but what is the connection between the Fall—which is the origin of all evil and suffering—and natural disasters?

! **However** the Protestant theologian John Calvin (1509-1564) developed Augustine's theodicy to account for natural evil. He believed that 'the whole order of nature was subverted by the sin of man'. In other words he thought that the Fall threw Nature out of balance, in which case natural evil is in fact the result of human sin. If there had been no Adam and Eve (and hence no Fall), then there would be no natural evil.

(5) Animal suffering

Augustine's theodicy does not seem to be a very satisfying explanation of the existence of animal suffering, as if we accept Augustine's idea that evil entered the world through Original Sin, we might yet still be sceptical of the idea that animal suffering is fair or just—why would God allow animals to suffer (when they have no free will, and hence cannot choose to commit sins)? Augustine saw the suffering of animals (for example the antelope that is killed by the lion) as a result of the corruption of the natural order caused by the Fall.

(6) Evil is not a lack of good

Swinburne is sceptical of Augustine's characterisation of evil as a lack of goodness. In 'The Problem of Evil', he gives a couple of examples to illustrate his view:

(i) 'A headache is a pain, whereas not having the sensation of drinking is, for many people, mere absence of pleasure.'
(ii) 'The feeling of loss in bereavement is an evil involving suffering, to be contrasted with the mere absence of the pleasure of companionship.'

Swinburne's point is that headaches and feelings of loss are not absences of goodness, but are rather *actual* pains (they are actual mental states for which we suffer). The implication is that we should think of evil not as **privatio boni** but rather as having a *positive* existence that Augustine fails to account for, in which case his theodicy fails to relieve God of responsibility for the existence of evil in the world.

> o thinkpoint o
> Which of these criticisms is the strongest? Which the weakest? Why?

Irenaean Theodicy

Whereas Augustine's theodicy is a soul-deciding theodicy, Irenaeus developed a **soul-making theodicy**. He held that God created the world with evil in it and this was the best world he could have made given that he wants us to develop morally and spiritually. This idea is captured in John Keats's expression that the world is a 'vale of soul-making'.

Irenaeus thought that we are created in **God's image**, and are immature and imperfect, although we do have the potential for improvement. And it is only by encountering evil and suffering in the world that we can develop morally and spiritually, and grow into **God's likeness**. Irenaeus said that through this process, we become 'children of God'.

God created humans with **free will** so that we could make moral choices, and respond in good or bad ways to the suffering that we see in the world. In this way, Irenaeus thinks that evil and suffering are necessary if we are to fulfil our purpose (i.e., to grow into God's likeness). However, our life on Earth is just the beginning of our development as we can only achieve moral and spiritual perfection in the afterlife, and we can achieve redemption through our actions—by responding to evil in the right ways. Irenaeus believes that God does not interfere when we make bad choices because he wants us to take responsibility for our own actions.

John Hick

In the 20th century, the English philosopher John Hick developed the Irenaean theodicy in his *Evil and the God of Love*.

Hick agreed with Irenaeus that we need to encounter evil and suffering in order to develop morally and spiritually (and work towards God's likeness). He illustrated this idea with the Christian virtue of **love**:

> 'the capacity for love would never be developed, except in a very limited sense of the word, in a world in which there was no such thing as suffering.'

So the idea is that we cannot become loving beings without making the right choices in the face of suffering (we can only demonstrate **agape**—impartial love for humanity—if we are presented with an opportunity to show it, and those opportunities only arise when we encounter human suffering). Hick concluded:

> 'A world without problems, difficulties, perils, and hardships would be morally static. For moral and spiritual growth comes through response to challenges; and in a paradise there would be no challenges.'

Hick thought that Irenaeus' theodicy is essentially correct. He argues that developing into a good person is far more satisfactory than having goodness already built in from the start (c.f. Augustine's theodicy). So if we are to develop morally then there are three conditions that must be met:

(i) We cannot have been created as morally and spiritually perfect beings;

(ii) God cannot intervene in our moral decision-making;

(iii) The world cannot be an earthly paradise.

That the world contains evil and suffering is, for Hick, a crucial aspect of the theodicy since it allows us the greatest chance to grow morally and spiritually. This is why the theodicy is described as a **soul-making** theodicy: because the world contains evil and suffering, it is perfect for our moral and spiritual growth.

For this reason, defenders of the Irenaean theodicy conclude that the world is better for containing evil and suffering than it would be if it contained none such. Gottfried Leibniz described this world as **the best of all possible worlds** as it is the creation of a perfect God.

> ○ thinkpoint ○
> What do you make of Leibniz's idea? Find out more about Leibniz's philosophical theories.

Strengths

(1) Possibilities for human development

In *Is There a God?*, Swinburne thinks that the fact that the world contains evil and suffering is a good thing for humans, as it gives us opportunities for moral and spiritual growth.

He gives the example of physical pain:

> 'A particular natural evil, such as physical pain, gives to the sufferer a choice—whether to endure it with patience, or to bemoan his lot. His friend can choose whether to show compassion towards the sufferer, or to be callous.'

He draws on Aristotle's idea that in order to *become* good people, we need to put ourselves in situations whereby we have the opportunity to *do* good, and by doing so, we improve as human beings (however, if we *fail* to do good when the opportunity arises, then we do not improve). This is what Swinburne means when he writes that:

> '… humans are so made that they can form their characters.'

So to *become* charitable (which is a good moral virtue to possess), we need to face situations whereby we can freely choose to perform charitable acts—and this requires some suffering to exist. In which case Irenaeus was right that evil and suffering are good for us.

(2) There is more to life than the pursuit of pleasure

Swinburne holds that the atheist's arguments against the existence of God based on the existence of evil and suffering contain a significant flaw. He points out that the arguments seem to be based on the idea that **pleasure** is the highest value in our lives, and that anything that frustrates our pursuit of pleasure is hence a bad thing. He argues that our lives can be much richer than this if we focus on our 'great responsibility for ourselves, each other, and the world'.

Swinburne supports his view with a version of Robert Nozick's **pleasure machine** criticism of hedonistic varieties of Utilitarianism; the conclusion of which shows that what really matters to us is not simply the pursuit of pleasure.

(3) No qualification of God's nature

Supporters of Irenaeus' theodicy argue that it is successful in its aim of reconciling the existence of evil (and suffering) and the existence of the God of classical theism without qualifying God's nature. The key to this is that we must realise that evil and suffering are *not* bad for us, but rather are essential for us if we are to fulfil our purpose.

> o think point o
>
> Can you think of any more strengths of the Irenaean Theodicy?

Criticisms

(1) Suffering of innocents

The first question that we need to raise in relation to the Irenaean theodicy is, 'Why do innocent people suffer?' It seems unfair and unjust that innocent children should have to starve in the famines of sub-Saharan Africa for people in MEDCs to cultivate the virtue of charitable giving. It seems wrong that innocent sufferers should exist as a means to an end, and we would expect a benevolent God to treat all humans with fairness.

! **However** this apparent problem is countered with the idea that all humans will go to Heaven, so the short period of suffering an innocent might undergo on Earth will be off set by an eternity in paradise. Hick responded this way in *Evil and the God of Love*:

> '… this infinite future good will render worth while all the pain and travail and wickedness that has occurred on the way to it.'

(2) A lack of justice

So, according to Hick, everyone will get to Heaven. But, it is argued, what is then the point of freely choosing to do the right thing in this life? It makes no difference in the long run. This criticism is that the theodicy entails that God is not just.

! **However** Hick maintained that the fact that everyone will be received into Heaven is a demonstration of God's love and benevolence. He argued that the idea of some people being condemned to Hell has no place in an adequate Christian theodicy.

(3) Animal suffering

We might be satisfied that the Irenaean theodicy can explain and justify the existence of human suffering, but what about the suffering of animals? The problem seems to arise because the traditional view of animals is that they are not ensouled, and hence do not have an afterlife.

! **However** Swinburne holds that in fact most animals are not capable of suffering to anything like the same degree as are humans. He argues that whereas we can suffer simply by thinking about the suffering that exists in the world, other animals suffer only hunger, tiredness and dying (the last of which is a short-term pain).

> o think point o
> What kinds of pain can we feel that animals cannot?

(4) Magnitude of suffering

We might be able to understand that we need to encounter some evil and suffering in order for us to be able to choose to do the right thing, but why is there so much evil and suffering in the world? This is sometimes called the **problem of immense suffering**: why did 6.5 million Jews have to die in the Holocaust rather than a much smaller number? Wouldn't rescuers such as Raoul Wallenberg and Oscar Schindler have been able to demonstrate their goodness in the face of far less evil? In essence, this is an attack on Leibniz's idea that this world is **the best of all possible worlds**: wouldn't a world that contained some suffering (but less than the world actually contains) be a better world?

> o think point o
> Does the Holocaust prove that this is not the best of all possible worlds? Why?

(5) Love

In his *The Concept of Prayer*, D.Z. Phillips (1934-2006) argued that if God really loved us, then he would not permit any suffering to occur. Suffering, for Phillips, is never the outcome of love.

! **However** we have seen that defenders of the Irenaean theodicy have tried to show that the existence of suffering is good for us. They would argue that by allowing us opportunities to grow morally and spiritually, God demonstrates his love for us.

(6) Moral evil

We might think that the Irenaeus–Hick theodicy explains why there is suffering in the world, but there remains a problem surrounding the existence of moral evil. We have not yet been given an explanation for why people choose to cause suffering to others.

! **However** Hick did response to this challenge, and this part of his theodicy is called the Free Will Defence.

The Free Will Defence

In *Evil and the God of Love*, Hick developed what is called the Free Will Defence to explain the existence of moral evil. He argued that the following three statements are true:

(i) God's omnipotence does not mean that he can produce something that is logically impossible.

(ii) It is necessary to be a person that we have free will.

(iii) An essential part of having free will is being able to choose to perform the morally wrong thing.

Building on Irenaeus' idea that God does not interfere with our choice-making, Hick described God as remaining at an **epistemic distance**—meaning that he does not reveal himself in a way that would force us all to believe in him. Rather, belief in God must be founded in faith. If God were to force his will on us by compelling us to always make the right choices, then this would be one way of revealing himself to us, and so God refrains from doing so, and thus maintains an epistemic distance. The consequence of this is that we have to decide for ourselves how to act, and sometimes we will make the right choice, and sometimes we will make the wrong one.

Hick argued that God does not want a world populated by robots that are all pre-programmed to believe in him and that automatically do the right thing, but instead God wants a world in which **autonomous** beings freely make choices. Hick concluded that because of this, God created a world that would appear to us *etsi deus non daretur* (as if there were no God).

Strength

Explanation of moral evil

The Free Will Defence seems a convincing explanation for why people choose to perform evil acts, and why an omnipotent God does not intervene to prevent them.

! However the **problem of immense suffering** seems to be an issue here: couldn't God act sometimes to prevent great moral evil (the Holocaust perhaps), whilst at the same time not intervening so as to take away our free will?

Well, Hick argued, if God intervened to prevent the greatest instances of evil, then he would have to intervene to prevent lesser evils, as we would then say that *they* were the greatest kinds of evil as we would know of no worse evils. This **slippery**

slope argument ends with God preventing *all* evil and suffering, which then removes the opportunity for moral growth, and reduces humans to mere robots (according to Hick). And it is for this reason that God did not prevent the Holocaust from happening, even though it caused such immense suffering:

> o think point o
> Can you give another slippery slope argument?

> 'These events were utterly evil, wicked, devilish and, so far as the human mind can reach, unforgivable; they are wrongs that can never be righted, horrors which will disfigure the universe to the end of time, and in relation to which no condemnation can be strong enough, no revulsion adequate. It would have been better—much much better—if they had never happened. Most certainly God did not want those who committed these fearful crimes against humanity to act as they did.'

Criticism

The Flew–Mackie challenge

Antony Flew accepted the first two claims of the Free Will Defence, but he thought that the third was false. As he wrote in his 'Divine Omnipotence and Human Freedom':

> 'Omnipotence might have, could without contradiction be said to have, created people who would always as a matter of fact freely have chosen to do the right thing.'

This objection seems to be based on the idea that free will involves being able to freely choose between two options, but that there is no need that one of those options is morally wrong. Therefore, God could have created humans with the character to only ever freely choose to do the right thing.

Mackie supported this criticism by pointing out that the choice God faced was not between: (i) creating robots lacking free will; and (ii) creating humans who sometimes freely choose evil over good. Mackie's point is that there is a third alternative: God could have created humans who always freely choose good over evil (and this would have been a better creation).

! **However** Hick argued in response to this challenge that if God had created humans that always chose to do the right thing, then the relationship between God and humans would be analogous to that between a hypnotist and his patient. The problem that Hick saw in the creation of this kind of human is that in just the same way as she would be incapable of choosing evil over good, she would have no choice in loving and worshipping God, in which case she would be incapable of having an 'authentic personal relationship with [God]'.

! A second response to the Flew–Mackie challenge comes from Swinburne who argues that the creation of humans with free will, but who are incapable of choosing evil over good, is not a logical possibility, and hence not something that God could have done (since God's omnipotence does not mean that he can do the logically impossible (see Chapter One)). Swinburne writes:

> **○ thinkpoint ○**
> Is the Flew-Mackie challenge convincing? Why?

'It is not logically possible—that is, it would be self-contradictory to suppose—that God could give us such free will and yet ensure that we always use it in the right way.'

Final Thoughts

As is the case with philosophical analysis, there seem to be more criticisms and problems with the two theodicies than strengths. But of course, this does not in itself mean that the theodicies both fail. In your evaluation, you will need to consider whether the theodicies are successful in meeting Mackie's challenge (that the existence of evil and suffering is logically incompatible with the existence of the God of classical theism) and Rowe's inductive argument (that the existence of evil and suffering makes it more likely that the God of classical theism does not exist). Ultimately, you might feel a pull in a particular direction, and then use your philosophical abilities to (i) support your belief; and (ii) deflect any potential criticisms.

We will close this chapter with the idea that perhaps the **suffering of innocents** will prove to be the stumbling block of *any* theodicy as expressed by Ivan in Book V, Chapter 4 of Dostoyevsky's *The Brothers Karamazov*:

> 'And if the sufferings of children go to swell the sum of sufferings which was necessary to pay for truth, then I protest that the truth is not worth such a price. I don't want the mother to embrace the oppressor who threw her son to the dogs! She dare not forgive him! Let her forgive him for herself, if she will, let her forgive the torturer for the immeasurable suffering of her mother's heart. But the sufferings of her tortured child she has no right to forgive; she dare not forgive the torturer, even if the child were to forgive him!'

Chapter Five
Miracles

Introduction

Miracles are an important area of study in the philosophy of religion, as they occupy a central role in classical theism. Theists tend to believe that God can perform miracles, and that through miracles God shows us that he exists and that he loves us. In this chapter we will study the philosophical ideas behind miracles, and consider the evidence that lends support to belief in miracles, and the reasons why some philosophers are sceptical.

We will begin this chapter with a review of some definitions of 'miracle'. As we shall see, there are a number of different definitions, and we may find that some are better than others (although what counts as a good definition might be up for discussion). It will be important to think about the attitude towards theism taken by those who create the definitions, as we might expect a theist to define miracles in a way that makes their existence highly plausible, whereas an atheist might define a miracle in such a way that creates difficulties in accepting that they could occur.

> o thinkpoint o
> Before reading further, how would you define 'miracle'?

As we move on to evaluative matters, we will encounter three distinct issues: (i) Do miracles occur? (ii) Is it rational to believe in miracles? (iii) How should we understand talk of miracles?

David Hume

Hume's definition

In Section X of *An Enquiry Concerning Human Understanding*, David Hume defined a miracle as an event that breaks the laws of nature. Hume started by stating that a miracle is ...

'... a violation of the laws of nature.'

A violation is something that breaks (or defies, or goes against) a law of nature. In order to understand what counts as such a violation, we first need to know what Hume understood a **law of nature** to be.

Laws of nature

Hume thought of laws of nature as *patterns* or *regularities* that can be seen in nature. He subscribes to the thesis of **empiricism**, according to which knowledge is ultimately rooted in our experience of the world. So the more empirical evidence we have for thinking that objects fall to the ground when dropped, the more confident we will be in believing that *gravity* is a *regularity* that can be seen throughout nature.

> **o thinkpoint o**
>
> We have seen Hume's criticisms of the Watchmaker argument in Chapter Two and of the Kalam argument in Chapter Three. How do these criticisms relate to his commitment to **empiricism**?

Now although what Hume thought of as a law of nature is not identical with our modern conception, we can at least identify the idea that miracles (if they occur at all) must be rare, since if something 'miraculous' occurred frequently, then it would be a *regularity*, and hence would fall under a law of nature rather than being a violation of a law of nature.

Hume himself gave an example of what he thought of as a law of nature: that 'all men must die'. And he thought that once we are dead, there is no coming back to life (this too is a law of nature). It would therefore count as a miracle, according to Hume's definition, if someone came back to life from being dead.

A refinement

Hume went on to develop his original definition of a miracle. He wrote that a miracle is ...

> '... a transgression of a law of nature by a particular volition of the Deity, or by the interposition of some invisible agent.'

As we have seen, a 'transgression of a law' is a *breaking* of a law, and now we see that Hume thinks that such a transgression requires God (or some other transcendent being) to bring about. This does not rule out the possibility of a person being involved in bringing about a miracle, but this would only be so if God were acting through the person in some way.

Aquinas

Aquinas' three categories of miracle

In his *Summa Contra Gentiles*, St Thomas Aquinas defined a miracle as something that is done ...

> '... by divine power apart from the order generally followed in things.'

He distinguished between three categories of miracle:

(i)   Something that could not have a natural cause;

(ii) Something that could have been caused naturally, but which has been brought about in a different (and unnatural) order or sequence;

(iii) Something that could have been caused naturally, but which has been brought about without any natural process.

(i) Something that could not have a natural cause

Aquinas considered these miracles to be of the highest rank. He gave the example of the parting of the Red Sea (Exodus 13-14). Aquinas thought that we are unable to comprehend how these events could occur without thinking of them as requiring God's intervention.

(ii) Something that could have been caused naturally, but which has been brought about in a different (and unnatural) order or sequence

The second order of miracle can be illustrated with the example of sight. Nature can cause someone to be able to have sight (it is not miraculous that most of us should have sight). But nature cannot cause a blind man to have sight—this requires God's intervention.

(iii) Something that could have been caused naturally, but which has been brought about without any natural process

The third kind of miracle includes things that can occur naturally, but have been caused without the usual natural processes. Aquinas gave the example of someone being cured of an illness through prayer. The person could have got better naturally, but God has intervened to effect a cure without the need for medication.

Miracles do not violate laws of nature

Timothy McGrew writes that what miracles of all three categories have in common is that they 'exceed the productive power of nature'. In other words, their occurrence cannot be put down to natural causes. However, Aquinas was careful to point out that miracles do not contradict the laws of nature as he was aware of the philosophical difficulties that this would bring (see the above section on Hume's definition).

In his *Summa Contra Gentiles*, Aquinas wrote that …

'… it is not contrary to nature when created things are moved in any way by God.'

And the reason he gave for this is that it is part of the natural world's *essence* to 'serve God'. So miracles are the result of God's intervention in the world, and yet—according to Aquinas—their existence does not entail the violation of genuine laws of nature. Aquinas drew on St Augustine's account of miracles according to which,

> 'We give the name "nature" to the usual common course of nature; and whatever God does contrary to this, we call a miracle. But against the supreme law of nature, which is beyond the knowledge both of the ungodly and of weak believers, God never acts, any more than He acts against Himself.'

In other words, Augustine held that there is a *supreme* law of nature that is never broken—even when God performs miracles—but this law is beyond our understanding. The laws of nature that we perceive as being violated by God when he performs miracles are only part of our 'human experience of the course of nature'. Since these 'laws' can appear to be broken, they cannot constitute the *supreme* law of nature.

Other key ideas concerning miracles

The task of coming up with a definition of some controversial concept like a miracle is clearly difficult, and some philosophers choose rather to highlight necessary conditions that must be satisfied if something is to count as a miracle.

Miracles must be the work of an interventionist God

> o thinkpoint o
>
> An important difference between theism and deism can be seen here. Investigate deism further.

Both Aquinas and Hume considered miracles to require God's intervention in the world. As we have seen in Chapter One, the God of classical theism is an omnipotent personal God. So this means that God is *able* to intervene in the world.

But we are still left with the question of *why* God would choose to intervene and cause a miracle. Richard Swinburne answers the question like this in *Is There a God?*:

> 'Natural laws are like rules, instituted by parents, schools, or governments … But loving parents will rightly occasionally break their own rules in answer to special pleading—it means that they are persons in interaction, not just systems of rules. And for a similar reason one might expect God occasionally to break his own rules, and intervene in history.'

So on Swinburne's account of miracles, God alters or suspends the laws of nature to demonstrate his loving (omnibenevolent) nature.

Miracles must lack naturalistic explanations

One way to go is to claim that it is necessary for an event to lack a naturalistic explanation in order for it to count as a miracle, that is that there is no plausible historical or scientific narrative that could be constructed to explain why the event happened. In this case, God's intervention is the <u>only</u> possible explanation for the event's occurrence.

! **However** in contrast to the idea that a miracle can have no naturalistic explanation, some theists argue that an event could count as a miracle even though there is a plausible naturalistic explanation for it. R.F. Holland uses the following story to illustrate this idea:

> A child's pedal car has got stuck on a train track, and the boy is so engrossed in trying to pedal free, that he fails to notice a train approaching from around a corner. His mother shouts to the boy, but he doesn't hear. The train stops just a few metres from the boy. The mother thanks God for the miracle, and continues to do so even though the train had stopped because the train driver had fainted (thus releasing the 'dead man's brake') due to a small blood clot lodging in his brain after a large lunch and an argument with a work colleague.

On the one hand, this story just looks like a string of coincidences that result in the survival of the child. Each step along the way has a naturalistic explanation, and therefore if miracles must be naturalistically unexplainable this *cannot* be a miracle. However, the fact that there are naturalistic explanations does not in itself rule out the possibility that one or more of the steps along the way were due to God's will. It is still open to believe that God willed the driver to faint at exactly the right time to save the boy's life *even though* there is a naturalistic explanation of why he fainted.

Holland defended an account of miracles whereby this kind of *coincidence* can count as a miracle. In 'The Miraculous', he writes,

> 'To qualify for being accounted a miracle an occurrence does not have to be characterizable as a violation of natural law.'

What is important on Holland's analysis is <u>not</u> that there is no naturalistic explanation, but rather that the coincidence can be **interpreted** as a miracle, and that it contains 'human significance'.

Significance

But what kind of significant consequence or outcome must something have if it is to count as a miracle? Certainly not any outcome would be significant in the right sort of way—for example winning the lottery would be significant for the person involved, but this is not the right kind of significance for the winning to count as miraculous. Richard Swinburne makes the following point in *The Concept of Miracle*:

> 'If a god intervened in the natural order to make a feather land here rather than there for no deep ultimate purpose, or to upset a child's box of toys just for spite, these events would not naturally be described as miracles.'

John Hick suggested that something does not count as a miracle if it 'fails to make us intensely aware of God's presence'. And he goes on to make it clear that the significance that a miracle must possess is **religious significance**. We might then think that in order for something to be a miracle, it must show us an aspect of God's nature (perhaps his omnibenevolence or omnipotence), and reinforce or renew faith.

Infrequent

It is sometimes argued that there couldn't be any miracles because of the existence of evil and suffering. So it is held that if God were benevolent and omnipotent, then he would intervene to prevent suffering. However, as Swinburne argues in *Is There a God?*, if God were to intervene each time something bad was about to happen, we humans would be absolved of our responsibilities, and then incapable of choosing well. He writes,

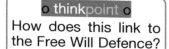
How does this link to the Free Will Defence? (See Chapter Four)

'[God] will not, however, intervene in the natural order at all often, for, if he did, we would not be able to predict the consequences of our actions and so we would lose control over the world and ourselves.'

Hence, given God's desire that we take responsibility for ourselves, miracles could <u>not</u> occur frequently.

Evaluation issue 1: are miracles possible?

Before we consider the rationality of believing in the existence of miracles, we should investigate some reasons for thinking that miracles are not simply unlikely, but that they are actually impossible.

Hume's definition revisited

One problem with thinking of a miracle as something that violates a law of nature is that this definition makes miracles not unlikely, but in fact *de facto* impossible. McGrew argues that this is a consequence of Hume's definition:

> 'On Hume's own "regularity" view of natural laws, it is difficult to see what it would mean for a natural law to be violated. If the natural laws are simply compendious statements of natural regularities, an apparent "violation" would most naturally be an indication, not that a supernatural intervention in the course of nature had occurred, but rather that what we had thought was a natural law was, in fact, not one.'

Hume thought that *humans cannot come back to life from being dead* is a law of nature because resurrection 'has never been observed in any age or country'. If someone did come back from the dead, this would entail that *humans cannot come back to life from being dead* is not in fact a law of nature, hence the observed resurrection is not a miracle. If it were established that an event *E* actually did occur, and *E* appeared to transgress a law of nature *L*, then according to the Humean analysis, this proves that *L* is not in fact a law of nature. Hence, there is no possibility that a miracle (understood as a violation of a law of nature) could occur. What would otherwise be a potential miracle is simply proof that a purported law of nature is not an actual law of nature.

! **However** to avoid ruling out the possibility of miracles simply by definition, Mackie developed Hume's account. In *The Miracle of Theism*, he wrote:

> 'The laws of nature … describe the ways in which the world … works when left to itself, when not interfered with. A miracle occurs when the world is not left to itself, when something distinct from the natural order as a whole intrudes into it.'

So, according to Mackie, resurrection *would* count as a miracle because resurrection would not occur without the intervention (or *intrusion*) of a divine being (God). Mackie believed that this is a more satisfactory way of defining a miracle (although he went on to argue that in fact they do not occur).

Scientism

Proponents of the thesis **Scientism** hold that if a phenomenon cannot be explained by science—if there is no scientific theory that explains its existence—then that phenomenon is not real. Therefore if a potential miracle lacks a scientific explanation, then it is not a real event.

! **However** it is not clear at all though that science has a monopoly on 'real' truth. Scientism has largely been discredited (perhaps the neatest argument

o thinkpoint o

What other ways of learning about the world do you rely on?

against scientism is that it seems as though the claim 'science is the only way of discovering truth' cannot itself be proved scientifically, in which case Scientism is **self-refuting**). This however does not in itself establish the reality of miracles.

Perhaps though we do not need as strong a view as Scientism to use science as a reason for the impossibility of miracles. If science deals in inviolable laws of nature, then this is enough to establish that miracles cannot exist—but only if a miracle is a violation of a law of nature.

!   However a **non-realist** will argue that laws of nature are simply useful ways of thinking about the world and making predictions about what will happen in the future. They can be changed to accommodate new data, and so should not be thought of as being 'set in stone'. (See p.84 ff. for more on **non-realism**.)

o thinkpoint o

Find out more about the non-realist understanding of science.

This non-realist move opens up the possibility of denying the existence of miracles once more, as when something seems to violate a 'law' of nature, all this shows is that the particular 'law' of nature was not actually a law at all (or at least an incomplete one). The miracle is then *absorbed* into the new 'law' of nature, and given a naturalistic understanding, in which case Hume's conclusion is substantiated. Holland made this point nicely in 'The Miraculous':

> 'Laws of nature can be formulated or reformulated to cope with any eventuality, and would-be miracles are transformed automatically into natural occurrences the moment science gets back on track to them.'

This pushed Holland to his *significant coincidence* account of miracles (see p.73).

Maurice Wiles

Theologian Maurice Wiles (1923-2005) argued that the occurrence of miracles is actually inconsistent with the existence of the God of classical theism. There are two arguments that he used to support his conclusion. Although Wiles himself did not set his first argument out exactly in the way that follows, I think this is a good way of understanding his point.

Wiles' first argument

Premise 1   All the natural laws within the universe were created in a single act in accordance with God's will.

Premise 2   A miracle is a violation of a natural law.

Premise 3   If God would violate a natural law, then God's will has changed.

Premise 4   God's will is unchanging.

Conclusion₁   Therefore God would not violate a natural law.

Conclusion₂   Therefore there are no miracles.

Now it is clear that Wiles was not denying that God created the universe (in fact, the argument relies on the universe being God's creation). The point is that the occurrence of miracles is inconsistent with the qualities of the God of classical theism, namely his timeless nature (and his unchanging will as a direct consequence of this). The argument has a valid structure, and therefore we can only resist the conclusions by denying one (or more) of the premises. We might deny **premise 2**, perhaps by employing Aquinas' conception of a miracle.

!   **However** we might want to argue that a miracle *is* the result of God's will, but is <u>not</u> the result of intervention at the time of the miracle's occurrence. Hence the universe is still the result of a 'single act of God', and there is no need to explain the occurrence of a miracle in terms of God's will having changed—on this picture, in his act of creation, God determines miracles to occur at some (future) points in the universe's history.

Wiles' second argument

Wiles' second argument against miracles again highlights an apparent conflict between the existence of miracles and God's qualities:

Premise 1   It is only reported that God brings about *trivial* miracles.

Premise 2   If the reports about the *trivial* miracles are true, then God's interventions are arbitrary, and he is not worthy of worship.

Premise 3   If the reports about the *trivial* miracles are false, then God does not intervene in the world at all.

Conclusion   Therefore either God is not worthy of worship, or he does not intervene in the world.

This seems a complex way of expressing the argument, but I think that this version captures what Wiles intended. Wiles provided the following reason for his controversial first premise in *God's Action in the World*:

> 'It would seem strange that no miraculous intervention prevented *Auschwitz* or *Hiroshima*, while the purposes apparently forwarded by some of the miracles acclaimed in traditional Christian faith seem trivial by comparison.'

!   **However** we might want to be told just what a '*trivial* miracle' actually is. As we have seen, a miracle is something with a human or religious significance, and if we build this idea into the definition of a miracle, then it would be argued that it is an *a priori* truth that there is no such thing as a *trivial* miracle.

But perhaps this misses the point: Wiles was arguing that regardless of the human significance of any given supposed miracle, it pales into insignificance when compared with the kind of miracle that would have prevented the horrors of the Holocaust or the dropping of the atom bomb. And that God chose not to intervene on these occasions underwrites Wiles' confidence in his argument.

! **However** Wiles' argument could be undermined with the claim that it is possible to believe that there have been *significant* miracles (in Wiles' sense), which have not been reported. If a miracle had been performed to prevent the Holocaust, then there would have been no Holocaust, and we would not be aware that God had saved the lives of six million Jews—hence this *significant* miracle could not have been reported.

Evaluation issue 2: is it rational to believe in miracles?

Provided that we think that miracles are at least possible—that it is possible that there is a personal God who (occasionally) intervenes in the world—then our attention should turn to the **epistemological** question as to whether there are good reasons for believing in the occurrence of miracles. If there are good reasons for believing in miracles, and these outweigh the reasons for not believing in them, then we say that it is **rational** or **reasonable** to believe in miracles (and conversely if the reasons for denying miracles outweigh those for believing in them, then it is not rational to believe in miracles).

Arguments for rational belief in miracles

There are plenty of places to find reports of miracles, from the Bible (both Old and New Testaments), to Lourdes, to newspapers. Could such reports carry enough weight to persuade us that they are true reports such that we *ought* to believe them? This is the epistemological question as to whether it is rational to believe in miracles, and it is one that Richard Swinburne has sought to answer. We should note that Swinburne is *not* trying to prove the occurrence of miracles beyond doubt, but only that it is *reasonable* to believe that they have occurred.

An argument based on Swinburne's principle of credulity

If you were to witness a miracle (on your preferred definition), do we want to say that at least you have good reason for believing in miracles? We can use an idea developed by Swinburne to argue that it is rational to believe that things are the way you experience them. He calls this the **Principle of Credulity**. It can be expressed in the following way:

Principle of Credulity   It is reasonable to believe that things are as they seem, unless you have good evidence that you are mistaken.

So we have a *personal* argument that justifies rational belief in miracles:

Premise 1	I have had an experience of what seems to me to be a miracle.
Premise 2	It is reasonable for me to believe that if something seems to be a miracle, then it is a miracle (unless I have good evidence that I am mistaken).
Premise 3	I have no evidence to suggest I am mistaken.
Conclusion	Therefore it is reasonable for me to believe that a miracle has occurred.

An argument based on Swinburne's principle of testimony

And what if someone reports his or her experience to you? Do you have a good reason to believe in miracles on the basis of someone's testimony? Well, Swinburne argues that in general it is rational to accept what people report to be the truth. He calls this the **Principle of Testimony**.

Principle of Testimony	It is reasonable to accept what people report to be the truth, unless you have good evidence that they are mistaken or unreliable.

This is the foundation for an *inter-personal* argument for rational belief in miracles:

Premise 1	Someone, *S* reports that she has witnessed a miracle.
Premise 2	It is reasonable for me to believe that if *S* reports that she has witnessed a miracle, then a miracle has occurred (unless I have good evidence that *S* is mistaken or unreliable).
Premise 3	I have no evidence to suggest *S* is mistaken or unreliable.
Conclusion	Therefore it is reasonable for me to believe that a miracle has occurred.

! However, what distinguishes reports of miracles from reports of alien encounters? We might think that the following argument is a counter-example to the inter-personal argument:

Premise 1	Someone, *S* reports that he has seen an alien.
Premise 2	It is reasonable for me to believe that if *S* reports that he has seen an alien, then aliens exist (unless I have good evidence that *S* is mistaken or unreliable).
Premise 3	I have no evidence to suggest *S* is mistaken or unreliable.
Conclusion	Therefore it is reasonable for me to believe that aliens exist.

> o thinkpoint o
> How would you respond to this argument from testimony?

! **Furthermore** a sceptic would argue that given the state of our current scientific world-view, someone who believes in the explanatory power of science does in fact have a good reason not to accept either one's own experience or someone's testimony concerning a miracle (taken as something that violates a law of nature). The sceptic could argue that it might well have been rational to believe in miracles on the basis of experience two thousand years ago, but it isn't today. This kind of response was put forward by the twentieth century theologian Rudolf Bultmann in his *Kerygma and Myth*,

> 'It is impossible to use electric light and the wireless and to avail ourselves of modern medical and surgical discoveries, and at the same time to believe in the New Testament world of spirits and miracles.'

The idea is that it is rational to believe in scientific achievements, because we can see them all around us (electric lights and radios). And since science works on the premise that there are inviolable laws of nature that explain *why* electric lights and radios work, it is therefore **irrational** to also believe in things that contradict these laws, such as miracles. Therefore the third premise in the arguments from credulity and testimony are false.

This criticism could be countered by adopting an account of miracles that does not require us to suspend our rational belief in scientific laws, such as Holland's *significant coincidence* account.

Swinburne's argument from history

Swinburne goes on to argue that there may be concrete historical evidence that supports the occurrence of miracles. In *Faith and Reason*, he writes that the evidence to establish the occurrence of a miracle would be ...

> '... of the same kind as the evidence for any other historical event. There is the evidence of one's own senses, the testimony of others (oral and written) and the evidence of traces ...'

So the evidence he has in mind includes the effects of the purported miracle. If there were effects that resisted naturalistic explanation, then we might think that there is good evidence for belief in miracles. We might think that Saul's conversion on the road to Damascus (Acts 9) had such effects (his evangelism), the **best explanation of which** involves God's miraculous intervention.

> o think**point** o
>
> Research the historical evidence for a selection of ancient and modern reported miracles.

Arguments against rational belief in miracles

If miracles *cannot* possibly occur, then it would be irrational to belief in them, but it would also be irrational to believe in miracles if there were good and compelling reasons for <u>not</u> believing in them. In this section we will consider why David Hume argued that it is not rational to believe in miracles.

Hume

As we have seen, Hume was an empiricist, and his scepticism of miracles was rooted in what he saw as a lack of evidence for our believing in them. Hume accepted that we can in general have good reasons for believing based on the testimony of others. So if I tell you that there is a woodpecker outside my window as I write this, you may feel that you are justified in believing that the author has just seen a woodpecker. However, Hume argued that testimony can never be sufficient for believing in miracles. He wrote that,

> '… no testimony is sufficient to establish a miracle, unless the testimony be of such a kind, that its falsehood would be more miraculous, than the fact, which it endeavours to establish …'

In other words, Hume thought that being told about a miracle is never a sufficient reason for believing that the miracle took place (unless not believing that the supposed miracle took place forces us to accept that an even less likely violation of a law of nature has taken place).

Note that this is not supposed to be an argument against the possibility of miracles, but rather an argument against rational belief in them (we can think of these objections as being raised against the *interpersonal* argument above). Hume provided four reasons for accepting his sceptical conclusion.

(i) Too few reliable witnesses

Hume's first point was that no miracle has ever been reported by enough *reliable* witnesses. He wrote:

> '… there is not to be found, in all history, any miracle attested by a sufficient number of men, of such unquestioned good-sense, education, and learning, as to secure us against all delusion in themselves; of such undoubted integrity, as to place them beyond all suspicion of any design to deceive others; of such credit and reputation in the eyes of mankind, as to have a great deal to lose in case of their being detected in any falsehood; and at the same time, attesting facts performed in such a public manner and in so celebrated a part of the world, as to render the detection unavoidable: all which circumstances are requisite to give us a full assurance in the testimony of men.'

So if a report of a miracle is to be trusted, there must be a sufficient number of people who agree that the miracle took place, and—in order to count as reliable—these people must have: (i) intelligence; (ii) no delusions; (iii) integrity; and (iv) a good reputation. In addition, the reported miracle must have been a public event in a place where it could not be missed.

! **However** there are some problems with this set of conditions. First, Hume nowhere explained what a 'sufficient number of men' is. 'Sufficient' here means 'enough', but we are not told how many people are needed for us to accept their testimony. Second, if we only trusted the testimonies of people who we know satisfy the four *reliability conditions*, we would find it very difficult to believe the testimonies of anyone. Our practical needs mean that we accept testimonies from people without establishing whether the reliability conditions are satisfied.

A follower of Hume could respond by arguing that in everyday life, we don't need the same level of assurance as we do when we are considering the possibility of miracles, that the need to establish *reliability* is variable depending upon what is claimed to be the case, and since the existence of miracles would ground a belief in a divine being (according to Hume's definition), this is an important issue, and so needs a careful and cautious approach (whether or not you believe that I did see a woodpecker is really neither here nor there).

(ii) Miracles tend to be reported by religious people

Hume's second point was that we have good reason to be suspicious of those who claim to have witnessed a miracle:

> 'A religionist may be an enthusiast, and imagine he sees what has no reality: he may know his narrative to be false, and yet persevere in it, with the best intentions in the world, for the sake of promoting so holy a cause ...'

Here the idea is that, for example, a Christian has a good reason to report a miraculous event (even though she knows it not to have occurred) because this can then be used to strengthen another's faith. The other side of the coin is that we, according to Hume, are inclined to be 'willing hearers'. This means that we suspend our rationality too readily, are too willing to accept stories that capture our imagination—especially when the testimony is presented in a convincing way.

! **However** this seems a bit too quick if the idea is that all reports of miracles are motivated by a desire to promote the religion. Even if we accept that Hume was right to warn against being *too willing* (or gullible) in accepting testimonies, this does not mean that religious believers cannot be reliable (according to the criteria in the previous section).

(iii) Miracles tend to be reported in primitive countries

The third reason that Hume presented against the acceptance of reports of miracles is that these testimonies originate in primitive and uncivilised countries. He wrote that miracles are …

> '… observed chiefly to abound among ignorant and barbarous nations; or if a civilized people has ever given admission to any of them, that people will be found to have received them from ignorant and barbarous ancestors …'

! **However** during Hume's own time (the 18th century) miracles were reported in countries such as France, Spain and Italy—and these would certainly not count as 'ignorant and barbarous nations'. The Enlightenment was in full sway at this time across Europe, and although Enlightenment thinkers certainly did much to change attitudes to religion by undermining much of the traditional authority of religion, religious sentiment was not altogether quashed.

It may be that Hume was intending to cast doubt on reports of miracles that pre-dated the Enlightenment (hence the clause concerning 'ignorant and barbarous *ancestors*' in the above passage). If we think of the Enlightenment in Kant's terms, as 'mankind's final coming of age, the emancipation of the human consciousness from an immature state of ignorance and error', we can place Hume's attack as part of the awakening: we should be cautious about pre-Enlightenment beliefs, and subject them to scrutiny and reason.

(iv) Conflicting claims

Hume's fourth point was that the existence of a 'Christian' miracle renders other religions false just as a genuine miracle attributable to Vishnu would disprove the existence of the Christian God. He argued that there is no good reason to suppose that Christian reports of miracles are any more reliable than those of Hinduism (or indeed any other religion), and hence no such testimony can ever be accepted.

! **However**, as Hume acknowledged, this argument relies on the idea that a difference between two religions represents a *contradiction* such that both religions cannot be correct regarding this difference. It could be argued that it is the same divine being who causes both Christian miracles and Hindu miracles, and it just happens to be that he reveals himself in different ways. If this were so, then believing in both kinds of miracle is not a contradiction.

It could be argued in response that this *assimilation* approach to religions reduces important theological differences between religions to insignificance, thus ignoring what is interesting and unique about each religion.

The falsificationist argument against miracles as *significant coincidences*

As we remember, Holland developed an account of miracles according to which a miracle is something that can be interpreted to be a miracle (recall his 'boy on the train tracks' miracle). There are then two ways of viewing this episode: either as a significant coincidence (i.e., as a miracle) or as just a plain coincidence. The boy's mother in the story is reported as maintaining her belief that the stopping of the train was a miracle even though she learns about the naturalistic explanation (concerning the train driver's health).

We can use Antony Flew's theory of **falsification** to argue that Holland's analysis means that belief in miracles is irrational. According to falsificationism, a belief is meaningless if there is no evidence that the believer would accept for giving up and rejecting the belief.

The mother then, according to the falsificationist, holds a meaningless and irrational belief in the sense that she does not accept the evidence that we would normally think of as showing that a miracle had not taken place.

! **However** R.M. Hare (1919-2002) responded to Flew's ideas. He argued that there are different ways of seeing and interpreting the world, and these frameworks he named **bliks**. The mother sees the stopping of the train as a miracle because she interprets the events from within her religious blik. Within this way of seeing the way, the naturalistic explanation for the stopping of the train does not count as evidence against it being a miracle, in which case her belief is not meaningless and irrational. Flew's argument is countered because different bliks have different accounts of what counts as evidence for accepting and rejecting beliefs. Hare argued that Flew has missed the point because he is applying the evidential standard of a *scientific* worldview within a *religious* framework.

We are clearly a long way from a simplistic understanding of what it is to believe in miracles, and much hangs on how we should understand talk of miracles. It is to this issue that we now turn.

Evaluation issue 3: an alternative approach (non-realism)

Before we end this chapter, we need to consider the view that has been held by some theologians such that reports of miracles are *not* to be thought of as reports of events that have actually happened. Certainly the *standard* view (and the one implicitly adopted in this chapter thus far) is that when we say that miracles exist, we are committing ourselves to the real existence of miracles (on whichever is your preferred definition). Philosophers call this a **realist** approach to miracles.

The alternative to this is to adopt a **non-realist** understanding of miracles. According to non-realism, we should not think that talk of miracles is 'straightforward' in the way that talk of apples and oranges is straightforward. Whereas 'apples exist' may be taken literally, 'miracles exist' should not. We shall consider two non-realist ways of thinking about miracles.

Miracles as myth

The idea that talk of miracles is not straightforward is not a new one. In the 19th century, Christian scholar D.F. Strauss argued in his *The Life of Jesus, Critically Examined*, that the New Testament miracles should be understood as myths. He denied that they actually happened, and that they feature in the Gospels to encourage belief that Jesus fulfilled **Messianic Prophecies**. This is a non-realist view as Strauss was suggesting that we can understand talk of miracles without committing ourselves to their existence. According to this non-realist approach, the purpose of a miracle-testimony is not to persuade you of the occurrence of a miracle, but rather to communicate some deep religious truth.

> o thinkpoint o
> Find out what a myth is. What do you think about the idea that the New Testament is a myth?

Like Strauss, the theologian Rudolf Bultmann believed that the New Testament miracles are myths. He defined myth as …

> '… the mode of representation in which the unworldly, the divine, appears as worldly, human, and the other-worldly as this-worldly.'

As we have seen, he denies that it is rational to believe in both the existence of miracles and science. Bultmann argued that we need to **demythologise** the Bible (i.e., strip away the myths) in order to be able to recognise the core religious truths (**kerygma**) that the mythical stories of miracles contain. What is important is not the myth itself, but rather the spiritual truths contained within it.

> o thinkpoint o
> Find out what Bultmann thought the core religious truths are that can be found within in the New Testament.

! **However** other theologians have expressed concern with Bultmann's view, as it seems to **secularise** the Bible. It could be argued that by discarding the accounts of miracles in the New Testament, the very religious truths that this process is supposed to reveal are lost (including perhaps what we might think of as fundamental Christian beliefs about Jesus' divinity).

Ludwig Wittgenstein

In the 20th century, no philosopher was as influential as Ludwig Wittgenstein (1889-1951). In his later work he introduced the concept of **forms of life** to explain the existence of different ways of seeing and interpreting the world. We can think that theism and atheism are different forms of life—different ways of seeing the world. So whereas the theist sees an event as a miracle, the atheist sees it as, say, a fortuitous coincidence.

If we recall R.F. Holland's example (see p.73), there is a wholly plausible naturalistic explanation as to how the train stopped before hitting the child. But, and this is the important point, a follower of Wittgenstein would hold that the naturalistic and 'super-naturalistic' accounts can both be correct: the two accounts are not contradictory, as they are found in different forms of life.

Followers of Wittgenstein argue that there is no way of determining which is the "true" or "best" way of seeing the world: there are simply different ways. There is no way of stepping outside some form of life or other in order to make an *objective* judgement. Of course, an atheist scientist will deny the possibility of miracles, but this denial originates from within the scientific form of life, and when we see the world as an atheist scientist does, it is true that miracles do not happen. Followers of Wittgenstein think that the concept of **truth** is applicable here, but we should not think that there is any truth independent of a form of life: there is no *objective* truth, but only truth relative to a form of life.

! **However** some philosophers are concerned that this view trivialises the notion of truth, and that we need a sense of *objective truth* in order to make sense of the world. As such, science is held up as a method for discovering the 'real truth' about the world, and since miracles are not part of the scientific worldview, they do not exist.

See the previous criticism of *Scientism* for a response to this kind of objection (pp.75-6).

Final Thoughts

We have encountered the **Principle of Parsimony** in previous chapters. A theist would argue that a miracle could be the simplest explanation of the phenomena, in which case, the existence of God is concluded. On the other hand, according to **Ockham's Razor** (the principle of ontological parsimony), if there is a satisfactory naturalistic explanation of an 'apparent' miracle then there is no need to postulate God's intervention. Of course, Ockham's Razor only applies if there is indeed a convincing naturalistic explanation for the apparent miracle.

Bibliography

Anscombe, G.E.M. (1974) 'Whatever has a beginning of existence must have a cause', in Davies (2000).

Aquinas, T. (1905) *Summa Contra Gentiles*, edited by J. Rickaby (London: Burns and Oates).

Aquinas, T. (1991) *Summa Theologiae A Concise Translation*, edited by T. McDermott (Christian Classics).

Aristotle (2004) *The Metaphysics* (Penguin Classics).

Aristotle (2008) *Physics* (Oxford: World's Classics).

Boyle, R. (1979) *Selected Philosophical Papers*, edited by Stewart M.A. (Manchester: MUP).

Collins, R. (1999) 'The Fine-Tuning Design Argument', in Murray, M.J. (ed) (1999) *Reason for the Hope Within* (Grand Rapids, MI: Eerdmans).

Copleston, F.C. (1948) 'A Debate on the Existence of God', URL = http://www.ditext.com/russell/debate.html.

Craig, W.L. (1979) *The Kalam Cosmological Argument* (London: Macmillan Press).

Craig, W.L. (1980) *The Cosmological Argument from Plato to Leibniz* (London: Macmillan Press).

Crick, F. (1990) *What Mad Pursuit* (London: Penguin).

Darwin, C. (2003) *Autobiography* (Cambridge: Icon Books).

Davies, B. (1993) *An Introduction to the Philosophy of Religion* (Oxford: Oxford University Press).

Davies, B. (2000) *Philosophy of Religion: a guide and anthology* (Oxford: OUP).

Davies, B. (2006) *The Reality of God and the Problem of Evil* (London: Continuum).

Dawkins, R. (2006) *The Blind Watchmaker* (London: Penguin).

Dawkins, R. (2001) *River out of Eden* (London: Phoenix).

Dostoyevsky, F. (2003) *The Brothers Karamazov* (London: Penguin).

Eddy, Mary Baker (1875) *Science and Health with Key to the Scriptures* (Boston: Christian Science Publishing Company).

Edwards, P. (1959) 'Objections to Cosmological Arguments', in Davies (2000).

Flew, A. (1972) 'Divine Omnipotence and Human Freedom' In Flew, A. and MacIntyre, A. (eds), *New Essays in Philosophical Theology* (London: SCM Press).

Garcia, L. (1999) 'Teleological and design arguments', in Quinn & Taliaferro (1999).

Hick, J. (1973) *God and the Universe of Faiths* (Oxford: Oneworld Publications Ltd).

Hick, J. (2010) *Evil and the God of Love* (New York: Palgrave Macmillan).

Himma, K.E. 'Design Arguments for the Existence of God', *Internet Encyclopedia of Philosophy*, URL = < http://www.iep.utm.edu/design/>.

Hoffman, J. & Rosenkrantz, G. (1999) 'Omnipotence' in Quinn & Taliaferro (1999).

Holland, R.F. (1965) 'The Miraculous' in *The American Philosophical Quarterly* vol. 2, no.1.

Howard-Snyder, D. (1999), 'God, Evil, and Suffering' in Michael J. Murray (ed) (1999) *Reason for the Hope Within* (Grand Rapids, MI: Eerdmans).

Hume, D. (1975) 'Enquiry concerning Human Understanding' in his *Enquiries concerning Human Understanding and concerning the Principles of Morals*, edited by L.A. Selby-Bigge (Oxford: Clarendon Press).

Hume, D. (2008) *Dialogues and Natural History of Religion* (Oxford: OUP).

James, W. (1982) *The Varieties of Religious Experience* (London: Penguin Classics).

Kant, I. (1998) *Critique of Pure Reason* (Cambridge: CUP).

Kenny, A. (1969) *The Five Ways* (London: Routledge).

Leibniz, G. (1995) 'On the Ultimate Origination of Things' in his Philosophical Writings (London: Everyman).

McCabe, H. (2005) *God Matters* (London: Continuum).

McCloskey, H.J. (1960) 'God and Evil', in *Philosophical Quarterly*, vol. 10.

McGrew, T. 'Miracles', *The Stanford Encyclopedia of Philosophy* (Winter 2010 Edition), Edward N. Zalta (ed.), URL = <http://plato.stanford.edu/archives/win2010/entries/miracles/>.

Mackie, J.L. (1955). 'Evil and Omnipotence', in *Mind*, vol. 64.

Mackie, J. L. (1982) *The Miracle of Theism* (Oxford: Clarendon Press).

Mavrodes, G. (1999) 'Omniscience' in Quinn & Taliaferro (1999).

Mill, J.S. (2009) *Three Essays on Religion* (Broadview Press).

Paley, W. (2008) *Natural Theology* (Oxford: OUP).

Peterson, M., (1999), 'The problem of evil', in Quinn & Taliaferro (1999).

Peterson, M., Hasker, W., Reichenbach, B. & Basinger, D. (2007) *Philosophy of Religion: Selected Readings* (Oxford: OUP).

Peterson M., Hasker, W., Reichenbach, B. & Basinger, D., (2009) *Reason and Religious Belief* (Oxford: OUP).

Phillips, D.Z. (1965) *The Concept of Prayer* (London: Routledge and Kegan Paul).

Plantinga, A. (1977) *God, Freedom, and Evil* (Grand Rapids, MI: William B Eerdmans Publishing Co).

Plato, (1970) *The Laws* (Penguin Classics).

Plato, (2008) *Timaeus and Critias* (Penguin Classics).

Quinn, P. & Taliaferro, C. (eds) (1999) *A Companion to Philosophy of Religion* (London: Blackwell).

Ratzsch, D. 'Teleological Arguments for God's Existence', *The Stanford Encyclopedia of Philosophy* (Winter 2010 Edition), Edward N. Zalta (ed.), URL = <http://plato.stanford.edu/archives/win2010/entries/teleological-arguments/>.

Reichenbach, B. 'Cosmological Argument', *The Stanford Encyclopedia of Philosophy* (Winter 2010 Edition), Edward N. Zalta (ed.), URL = <http://plato.stanford.edu/archives/win2010/entries/cosmological-argument/>.

Rowe, W. (1979) 'The Problem of Evil and Some Varieties of Atheism', in *American Philosophical Quarterly*, vol. 16, no. 4.

Rowe, W. (1988) 'The Evidential Argument from Evil', in Peterson *et al* (2007).

Rowe, W. (1999) 'Cosmological Arguments', in Quinn, P. & Taliaferro, C. (1999).

Russell, B. (1948) 'A Debate on the Existence of God', URL = http://www.ditext.com/russell/debate.html.

Segal, R.A. (2004) *Myth: A Very Short Introduction* (Oxford: OUP).

Swinburne, R. (1971) *The Concept of Miracle* (London: MacMillan).

Swinburne, R. (1977) 'The Problem of Evil' in Brown, S.C. (ed) *Reason and Religion* (Ithaca: Cornell University Press).

Swinburne, R. (1981) *Faith and Reason* (Oxford: Clarendon Press).

Swinburne, R. (ed) (1989) *Miracles* (New York: MacMillan).

Swinburne, R. (2004) *The Existence of God* (Oxford: Clarendon Press).

Swinburne, R. (2010) *Is There a God?* (Oxford: Oxford University Press).

Taliaferro, C. 'Philosophy of Religion', *The Stanford Encyclopedia of Philosophy* (Spring 2011 Edition), Edward N. Zalta (ed.), URL = <http://plato.stanford.edu/archives/spr2011/entries/Philosophy-religion/>.

Tennant, F.R. (1928) *Philosophical Theology* (Cambridge: CUP).

Tooley, M. 'The Problem of Evil', *The Stanford Encyclopedia of* Philosophy (Spring 2010 Edition), Edward N. Zalta (ed.), URL = <http://plato.stanford.edu/archives/spr2010/entries/evil/>.

Vardy, P. (1999) *The Puzzle of God* (London: Fount).

Vardy, P. & Arliss, J. (2003) *The Thinkers Guide to God* (Ropley, Hants.: O Books).

Wiles, M. (1986) *God's Action in the World* (London: SCM Press).

Zagzebski, L. (2007) *Philosophy of Religion: An Historical Introduction* (Oxford: Blackwell).

Name index

Al-Kindi, 40

Anscombe, G.E.M., 43

Aquinas, St Thomas, 14, 15, 16, 24, 31, 33, 34, 35, 36, 37, 38, 39, 40, 42, 70, 71, 72, 77

Aristotle, 13, 14, 15, 33, 34, 37, 63

Augustine, 53, 56, 57, 58, 59, 60, 61, 62, 72

Boyle, Robert, 17, 18

Bultmann, Rudolf, 80, 85

Calvin, John, 61

Clarke, Samuel, 45

Collins, Robin, 26

Copleston, F.C., 38, 39, 40, 49, 50

Craig, William Lane, 40, 41, 42, 43

Crick, Francis, 23

Darwin, Charles, 22, 23, 29

Dawkins, Richard, 23

Dostoevsky, Fyodor, 68

Eddy, Mary Baker, 56

Flew, Antony, 30, 56, 67, 68, 84, 88

Hare, R.M., 84

Hick, John, 49, 51, 62, 63, 64, 65, 66, 67, 74

Holland, R.F., 73, 76, 80, 84, 86

Howard-Snyder, Daniel, 51

Hume, David, 20, 21, 22, 23, 24, 37, 42, 43, 48, 69, 70, 71, 72, 75, 81, 82, 83

Irenaeus, 57, 61, 62, 66

Kant, Immanuel, 30, 31, 40, 83

Kenny, Anthony, 35

Leibniz, Gottfried, 43, 44, 45, 46, 63, 65

Mackie, J.L., 47, 53, 54, 55, 57, 67, 68, 75

McCabe, Herbert, 58

McCloskey, H.J., 54, 88

McGrew, Timothy, 71, 75

Mill, J.S., 24, 55

Miller, Ed, 41

Newton, Isaac, 17

Nozick, Robert, 64

Name index